Terry Orlick PhD

Feeling Great

Teaching children to excel at living

Also by Terry Orlick:
The Cooperative Sports and Games Book
Every Kid Can Win
In Pursuit of Excellence
Nice on My Feelings: Nurturing the Best in Children and Parents

**New Edition!—previously released under
the title *Free to Feel Great***

C REATIVE
B OUND ◇

Published by Creative Bound Inc.
P.O. Box 424, Carp, Ontario
Canada K0A 1L0
(613) 831-3641

ISBN 0-921165-43-9
Printed and bound in Canada

Copyright © 1996 Terry Orlick

Book design by Wendelina O'Keefe
Cover photograph by Dugald Bremner/Tony Stone Images
Illustrations by Ari Niemi
Photograph of Terry Orlick by Pierre Bertrand

Canadian Cataloguing in Publication Data

Orlick, Terry, 1945-
    Feeling great: teaching children to excel at living

Rev. ed.
First ed. published under title: Free to feel great.
Includes bibliographical references and index.
ISBN 0-921165-43-9

  1. Children—Conduct of life. 2. Success. 3. Stress in
children. 4. Child rearing. I. Title. II Title: Free to
feel great.

HQ769.O75 1996   649'.1   C96-900001-4

Dedication

To Nadeane McCaffrey for your
continued support and for making
a difference in the lives of children—
towards a higher quality of life.

Acknowledgments

There are many people, young and old, who have stimulated my search for positive ways to improve the quality of human lives. Virtually every child with whom I have worked has become my teacher in some way. Those who are on a positive path inspire me to think of ways to free more people to step on this path. Those who are on a less positive path are constant reminders of the need to find effective ways to free more people to live truly meaningful and humanistic lives.

There are many people who have been influential in helping me get to the stage of presenting the ideas and activities in this book. The thousands of children, teachers and parents who helped us to create, assess and refine our activities within an elementary school setting. Nadeane McCaffrey, Children's Life Skills Study co-ordinator, Jennifer Cox, Marnie St. Denis, Louise Zitzelsberger, Jenelle Bonadie and Shaunna Taylor, who were instrumental in contributing ideas, time and passion to this project over the years, and many more for giving of themselves to improve the lives of children. The Social Science and Humanities Research Council of Canada (SSHRC) for helping support my research on cooperative values and positive life skills for children. My working colleagues in Sweden who were instrumental in distinguishing Sweden as the first country in the world to include relaxation training for all children as a regular part of their national school curriculum, and in particular Elisabeth Solin who has introduced our joint project "The Can-Swe program" into their school curriculum.

Creative Bound Inc., my inspired publishers for *Feeling Great* and *Nice on My Feelings,* who continue to provide me with a delightful, respectful and supportive publishing experience.

The 4- to 12-year-old children from our Feeling Great program for their various quotes used throughout the book.

Thank you all for keeping the magic in each day and for providing our children with some real hope for the future.

Terry Orlick

Feeling Great

The path to balanced excellence and joyful living
lies in living highlights.

The way to live more highlights
is to bathe in simple joys,
simple joys that are all around you
and within you.

Look closely and you will see them.
Stretch out your arms and you will touch them.
Open your heart to
embrace them.

Now is the time,
this is the place,
for living highlights.

Seize this moment to live
life's simple joys.
Dance with life. Embrace it.
Open yourself to its magic.

Create your own opportunities.
Walk forward in life—proudly, freely, playfully,
with your eyes and heart open
and your arms outstretched to the sky.

Table of Contents

Positive Beginnings

As parents and teachers there is no greater mission we can fulfill on this earth than teaching skills for positive living. Everything else depends on this—the state of our relationships, our health, our economy, the quality of our individual and collective lives, and life itself.

Our ultimate goal with children is to teach them positive perspectives that will enhance the quality of their lives and endure throughout their lifetime. There is a great advantage in beginning this process at an early age. Children who are taught to think positively and focus effectively will be well-equipped to pursue their goals and dreams, find joy in their experiences and direct the course of their own lives.

Children are highly capable of learning a variety of important life skills. They can apply these skills in virtually everything they do—play, games, sports, school, studies, art, music, dance, career developments, as well as within relationships and ongoing interactions at home and in the community.

You will provide a huge service to your children by teaching them positive life skills and stress control strategies *now*. The activities in this book are designed specifically to help you teach children to:

- Think positively
- Relax effectively
- Cope constructively with stress, conflict, anger and frustration
- Concentrate fully

- Recognize good qualities within themselves and others
- Find uplifting experiences (highlights) in each day
- Feel great about themselves
- Cooperate joyfully
- Use their imagination in positive ways
- Carry more positive perspectives into everyday transactions and pursuits

The overall goal of these activities is to free children to learn more effectively, live more joyfully and love more completely.

The activities in this book were developed from a deep commitment to meet the real needs of children, parents and teachers living through very challenging times. The activities have undergone extensive research with thousands of elementary school children. We spent ten years developing the activities and another three years testing them in the schools. Many children, along with their parents, teachers and principals have helped us to assess, refine and improve the overall quality and effectiveness of this program.

The impact of the *Feeling Great* activities has far surpassed our initial expectations. It has proven to be a highly effective program for teaching children critical skills for positive living. It has helped children learn to strengthen their confidence, cope effectively with stress, relax their minds and bodies, use their imagination in creative ways, channel their concentration, interact positively with others and feel great about themselves and their capabilities. It has resulted in less stress, more effective learning, and a greater sense of respect and harmony within and among children.

Children really enjoy the activities and apply these skills effectively in their daily lives. You can share these activities with your children at home or at school, repeating them often enough for children to gain competence at using them. When teaching children to excel at living, repetition is important.

You can do the activities together with your children at school, at home, in the outdoors or at bedtime. By participating in these activities your children will become surprisingly competent at living these important life skills.

Feeling Great and its soul mate (partner book) *Nice on My Feelings* provide the essential spirit, pathways and activities for teaching children skills for positive living. The activities are presented on the following pages. You can read the various scripts to your children (for relaxation, positive imagery, focusing and positive thinking) or you may prefer to sit back, relax and listen to the activities with your children on audio-tape. A *Curriculum Guide* and series of audio-tapes were created from the material in this book for teachers and parents who want a very simple and effective way to deliver this program to their children, day-by-day (see Resource section in this book).

Parents, teachers, and all those who interact closely with children can immediately put these activities to good use. Through your initiatives children will learn vital life skills— with joy and simplicity. You will be giving them the greatest gifts of life—skills that allow children, families and nations to excel at living.

Positive Thinking

Did you ever have a day where you got up on the wrong side of the bed?

No, I can't cause my bed goes right up against the wall. (7-year-old)

What is POSITIVE THINKING?

Like when Peter Pan goes to Never Never land and he has to think good thoughts to get there, in order to fly. (11-year-old)

When you're playing football and everyone's guarding you, you think that you can get through. (8-year-old)

Thinking I can do anything if I try! (9-year-old)

Thinking I will be nice to my friends. (10-year-old)

When you tell your friends you're going to make a clubhouse and you do! (8-year-old)

When you think right! (7-year-old)

Excellence in living, loving, working and playing, is made possible by developing the ability to think, dream and focus in positive ways. All worthy accomplishments are grounded in positive thinking. All positive emotions and human attributes, including self-confidence, happiness and personal excellence, are determined by the extent to which you think and act positively.

Positive emotions are incredibly uplifting and negative emotions are devastating—on performance, health, relationships, and our ability to concentrate or enjoy life. By teaching children to recognize positive things in their lives, we teach them to be open to opportunities, to think, feel and act in positive ways. By teaching them to generate positive emotions within themselves and others, we teach them to cope positively with negative emotions, to turn negatives into positives—these are the most essential lessons for creating a higher sense of respect, joyfulness, acceptance and belonging throughout life.

There are millions of talented children who have little or no self-confidence due to negative thinking, which originated from others, and was then self-inflicted. Negative thinking undermines everything. Children who view themselves negatively have learned to see themselves as limited and their world as limiting.

Have you ever been put down or treated with disrespect? How did it make you feel? How many times have negative actions or reactions from others made you feel unappreciated, unworthy, rejected or hopeless? How often has someone implied that you are useless, stupid, not good enough or incompetent? How many times have you been told that you *should have* done something different, better, earlier, later or faster? What does that do to *your* joy or *your* self-confidence? How often have you been negative with yourself, or spoken to yourself in a way that undermines your own confidence? Have you ever called yourself "useless," "stupid" or something more graphic that implies you are incapable, weak, incompetent, unworthy or a jerk?

The problem with negative thinking is that it destroys confidence, heightens anxiety, kills enjoyment and interferes with your chances of performing well, especially if you are already feeling vulnerable.

It is extremely important for children to feel good about themselves and their abilities. By teaching them to think and see positively, we free them to develop their talents, experience less anxiety and balance the abundance of negative input to which they will be subjected. Positive thinking enables children to grow with self-confidence and maintain a sense of perspective and positiveness throughout their lives.

You can free children to live life fully and experience life joyfully by helping them to develop positive life perspectives and positive mental skills at an early age. In simple ways, you can encourage them to look for the good things in themselves, in others and in their experiences each day. You can remind them to talk to themselves in positive ways, to recognize their own strengths, to "see" or imagine themselves as skilled, confident and capable. You can teach them to replace negative thoughts with positive thoughts, to find opportunities in everything and to act in positive and uplifting ways.

A good way to begin teaching children positive life perspectives is to be respectful and positive in your own interactions with them, and to introduce them to following uplifting activities.

Looking for Highlights

A highlight is something that makes you feel good, like giving your friend her birthday present. (5-year-old)

Highlights are things that let your good feelings come out each day. (7-year-old)

Highlights are the opposite of lowlights. (6-year-old)

Highlights are good things you can think of if you're feeling bad to make you realize it wasn't that bad a day. (12-year-old)

They let you taste a little bit of wonderful each day. (6-year-old)

Our research has clearly shown that when you teach children to look for highlights, they find more good things in each day, and as they find more good things, they begin to feel better and better about themselves. Looking for highlights is a great way to begin teaching children and adults to think positively and live more of life's simple joys. Recording highlights in a Highlight Book helps us to see the good in each day and enables us to maintain inner strength and perspective when experiencing setbacks. A Highlight Book is a simple log book or personal diary which focuses only on positive things. Children record positive events, positive experiences, positive comments, personal accomplishments or pluses for that day. This includes any simple pleasure, little treasure, joy, lift, positive feeling, meaningful experience, magic moment or anything that has lifted the quality of that day for that person. Children are asked to record or draw a few of these highlights each day, either before going to sleep, or during the day whenever they occur.

To begin this activity children are given a simple notebook, log book or diary which they decorate in a special way. They can create their own special cover with interesting drawings, colorful stickers or cut-outs from magazines. They may also buy a special book of their own choosing, or use our *Feeling Great Highlight Book* (see Resource section).

Looking for highlights places emphasis on noticing, recognizing, feeling, appreciating and recalling simple joys, many of which otherwise go unnoticed or unappreciated. The process of extracting and sharing highlights teaches children to look for good things, to enjoy simple pleasures and cherish simple treasures. It helps them realize that most of life's joys are of a very simple nature and well within reach, every day. Recording highlights encourages children and adults to look for "the positive" within themselves, their experiences and others. It helps them to recognize that many of life's simplest experiences provide the greatest sense of joy and fulfillment. In the beginning there may be a tendency to look for big highlights, but with encouragement children will also find little highlights which occur many times every day. Simple highlights may be experienced in a variety of ways, for example, through human contact, nature, play, personal accomplishments, relaxation, discoveries or positive sensations. Some highlights may only last a few wonderful seconds, but they can also endure over a lifetime.

Human Contact—a warm hug; a gentle smile; a positive comment; a good listener; shared laughter; a helping hand; a simple expression of respect, love, caring or appreciation; sharing special time with a loved one or good friend.

Contact with Nature—a beautiful beach, lake, stream, tree, flower, cloud, breeze or sunset; a thousand diamonds glistening on the water or sparkling on the snow; a bird soaring or respectful contact with an animal in a natural setting.

Play, Games, Sport—a joyful moment of playfulness, fun, laughter, movement, excitement, creation or interaction in play or games; playing with friends; a special feeling, or feeling special, while playing.

Personal Accomplishments—learning something new, accomplishing something you have been working at, setting a simple goal and completing it, finding a solution, feeling improvement, doing something well, doing your best or making a meaningful contribution.

Relaxation—a joyful moment of relaxation, calm or tranquillity; slowing things down; a quiet repose; a time-out for yourself or with a loved one to enjoy, relax or reflect.

Discovery—discovering something new, special or personally meaningful, for example, through interacting, observing, playing, performing, reading, listening, traveling or helping; creating something novel, interesting, fun or meaningful, for example, through imagining, reflecting, drawing, writing or working with your mind and hands.

Good Sensations—feelings of excitement; great sensations within your body; a nice hot shower, warm bath or Jacuzzi; a refreshing swim; a favorite drink, dessert or meal; the feel of wearing special clothing, perhaps a game uniform, or slipping into bed with clean, fresh, flannel sheets.

It is not necessary to always write down your highlights, although it certainly heightens your awareness of what they are and how to find them. Those who are not able to write, or who do not like to write, can draw pictures of their highlights or simply reflect back on the day, game or activity to re-experience highlights and share them with friends, teammates or family members. When you reflect upon, record or discuss highlights, they are more fully appreciated and tend to stay with you longer.

An important part of learning to live more simple joys lies in sharing highlights with others. Children can share their highlights with parents and parents can share their highlights with children either at the end of the day or just before they go to sleep ("What were your highlights today?"). It is a wonderful way to end the day on a positive note and set the stage for a positive tomorrow. In school, students can spend five minutes each day sharing highlights with classmates in small groups. Teachers can also share their highlights. Sharing highlights often becomes a highlight in itself. It is an uplifting experience for everyone because everything is focused on "the positive." It teaches people to dwell on positive things rather than negative things. It also opens the door for experiencing more highlights.

Sharing highlights is an excellent medium for positive communication, for understanding others and for seeing the good things within yourself. While sharing highlights, a great deal of learning occurs about what lifts people, what makes people feel good or valued and what makes life worth living. Within life's simple highlights are housed important lessons about positive communication and positive living. Highlights tell you how to create the conditions for more highlights within your own life, as well as within the lives of your children, family, students and loved ones.

Children can be asked to think of, share or write down in their Highlight Book: things I like, people I like, animals I like, people that make me feel good, things that make me feel good, things I'd like to do today, this week, this life, songs I like, comics or comic strips I like, movies/shows I like, sports/athletes I like, places/foods/desserts I like, qualities in people I like, qualities (good things) in me I like, dreams I would like to pursue. When you focus on looking at all the good things within you and the world around you, you begin to see yourself and your world in a more positive way.

In team situations, sharing highlights after practices and games is an effective way of promoting collective positive thinking. Even in losses or setbacks there are good things that happen, positive lessons to be learned and good reasons to believe in yourself and your teammates. Sharing highlights can be done verbally and reinforced with videotapes that highlight the good things that happened in the game. Sharing game highlights helps people recognize the good things and helps everyone remain positive about the future.

Highlight Games

The following highlight activities can be used in a variety of settings (at home, in school, in the gym and in the outdoors) to help children embrace the good things in life.

Highlight Circles—Each child is given the opportunity to share or act out a highlight within the group.

Highlight Charades—Children join together with one or two other children to act out their highlights. Before starting they are given a few minutes to discuss and plan their act. They then take turns acting out their highlights, and their friends, classmates or family members try to guess their highlights.

Highlight Pictures (Show and Tell)—Children draw or paint a picture of a highlight, and then share their picture with the group.

Highlight Pictionary—Players are divided into several small groups. Within their own group each child draws a highlight on the board or on a piece of paper for their teammates to guess.

Cooperative Highlight Egg Pass—Children write or draw a highlight on a small piece of paper and insert it into a plastic egg, envelop or empty match box. In circle, children pass their egg to the person on their left, each time you say "pass." When you say open, one at a time, the children share the highlight inside the egg they are holding. Children also enjoy trying to guess whose highlight they found.

Highlight Hunt—Children write or draw one highlight on a piece of paper. They then try to find other children who have had the same highlight. Children can also try to find people with different highlights.

Highlight Domain Scavenger Hunt—Within a group setting children are asked to find someone who has had different types of highlights. For example, find someone who had a highlight *Playing, Relaxing, In Nature, With Another Person, Tasting*, etc. Children move around finding people who experienced different highlight domains that day, and write their names down on a piece of paper.

Cooperative Highlight List—Children work together to think of as many highlights as they can and write them on a list. This is a cooperative effort and children are encouraged to add to the list over the course of the day, week, month or year as they think of new ones.

Highlight Bag/Highlight Jar—Each child writes or draws a personal highlight on a small piece of paper and places it in a special Highlight Bag or Jar. The Highlight Bag is left in the classroom and children are encouraged to add highlights to it during the day. If a child is having a bad day or needs a little lift he/she can be encouraged to look for a little highlight in the Highlight Bag/Jar.

Highlight Goals—Children set their own goals for increasing the number of simple highlights they experience, or the domains in which they experience highlights. For example, children can use their *Feeling Great Highlight Book* or index cards to write down simple highlights they would like to experience today or tomorrow, and then go out and "find" them.

Highlight Collage—Children create personalized Highlight Collages with magazine pictures, drawings or personal photographs. The collages can become a part of their log books or posters.

Highlight Collage Sharing—Each child is given an opportunity to share their Highlight Collage with the group. They explain the various highlights depicted in their collage.

Highlight Poems—Give children an opportunity to write a poem or story about highlights, or about their feelings when they experience highlights. Ask them to share their stories or poems with their family, friends or classmates.

Encourage the children to create their own highlight games, and to think of new ways to teach people about highlights, or to get people to live more simple joys.

Highlights

Happy and good
It's never bad
Great
Happiness is the key
Little things in life
It doesn't have to be big
Good and fun
Have them every day
The good things in life
Super special

– (9 year-old)

Games for Positive Thinking

The following activities are excellent for promoting positive self-esteem, positive thinking, positive action and interaction.

Sharing Things I'm Good At

Each child is asked to write down (or think of) at least five things that she is good at or that she likes about herself (e.g., I'm good at making friends, helping others, drawing, biking, swimming; I like my hair, the way I treat my friends, my life). The list should exclude anything negative (e.g., I'm good at not listening, I'm good at hurting others). If a negative statement does occur, simply request that it be replaced with something more positive and give a positive example.

Once each person has completed his or her own list of good things, the children sit in a circle and, in turn, share their good qualities with group members. Children are encouraged to sit or stand tall and share their good points with assurance and conviction. Ask them to stand tall and speak loud enough for everyone to hear. Children sitting around the circle should be instructed to show their respect and acceptance by "listening closely." As each person finishes sharing her good list, group members can clap to express their acceptance and appreciation. Adults joining in these activities should also take their turn in sharing their own good points.

It may take time for some of the children to stand tall and share their good points with conviction, but this is an important part of the learning process. Tell the children that it's good to be proud of the things they do well, and that it's okay to share their good points with others. Repeat the activity often enough for children to feel comfortable sharing their good qualities.

Occasionally there are children who cannot think of anything they do well. If this happens, ask other children in the circle to help think of things this child is good at (e.g., "you're good at being a friend," "reading," "helping," "skipping"). Children are very willing to help other children find some good things.

Another possibility for helping children recognize that they are good at some things is to give them a checklist containing many things that they are likely to do well. Let them tick off things they are good at and see if they can add to the list.

Put a check mark (√) next to each thing you are good at:

breathing	( )	wearing clothes	( )
seeing	( )	hugging	( )
hearing	( )	helping	( )
speaking	( )	art	( )
laughing	( )	learning	( )
sitting	( )	reading	( )
standing	( )	sleeping	( )
walking	( )	tasting good things	( )
skipping	( )	thinking	( )
biking	( )	enjoying nature	( )
running	( )	being a friend	( )
jumping	( )	doing nice things	( )
playing	( )		

Fill in other good things you are good at whenever you think of one:

_____ ( )
_____ ( )
_____ ( )
_____ ( )
_____ ( )
_____ ( )

Sharing Things Others Are Good At

We have spoken of sharing personal highlights and personal assets. In this activity each person shares what he or she feels are the good qualities of other people in the group. This works particularly well within families, close-knit teams and groups who know each other well. Only good things can be mentioned—nothing negative. It is always uplifting to hear others tell you about your strengths, your good points and things they appreciate or admire about you. You learn a lot about each other's qualities and about the good things that family members, teammates or classmates see in you.

When introducing this activity in school or camp settings, children are divided into groups of four or five. While sitting in their circle, one by one each child shares something positive or uplifting about a particular child—for example, one thing they like or admire about that person. When receiving a positive comment or compliment, children are encouraged to openly accept the compliment by responding with a warm and genuine "thank you." Consider spending a few moments at the end letting children exchange how they felt when they shared good feelings with their friends and heard good things about themselves from their friends.

Other options for this activity include sharing one good thing: about your team, teammate, mom or dad, family, friend, teacher, coach, school or community; or one good thing you did well today, someone else did well today, someone said or did that made you feel good today, you would like to do today, you would like to do with your life—a personal dream.

Eye Contact

This is a circle game with a positive twist. Players form a circle, stretch their arms out to the side so they can touch fingertips with the person on each side and drop their arms. The goal of the game is to make eye contact and then say something positive to as many other players as possible. As soon as two players "meet" with their eyes they both walk towards one another, shake hands, exchange greetings ("Hi, I'm Terry" — "Hi, I'm Lauren"), exchange positive comments ("I like your hat, Lauren"—"I like your smile, Terry"), and then exchange positions in the circle. Once they are back in the circle they immediately try to make mutual eye contact with another person. Many positive exchanges can occur at the same time if players focus intently on making eye contact. Positive comments can include anything that will be received in a positive way (e.g., I like your eyes, hair, shirt, voice, shoes, energy, the way you treat others or any other personal quality).

Act as if You Can

The chances of learning and performing skills well are greatly enhanced when children act as if they can do it—in their minds, in their body, and in the real world when they try it. Before children attempt skills, ask them to "act as if you can" by repeating to themselves "I can do this," and by imagining themselves doing it successfully. Then remind them to "act as if you can" just before they are about to do it. "Acting as if you can" is particularly important when children have doubts or worries about their own abilities. It allows them to step into the mind-set of a confident performer who walks tall and believes in his capabilities. It frees them, at least temporarily, from negative thoughts and failure images often associated with "I can't do it" or "I'm not that good," and allows them to focus on doing the skill. Thinking *I can do it*, and then focusing only on doing it, works much better than thinking I can't and worrying about not being able to do it. When the mind is positive and focused, anything is possible.

Act as if You Are

In this activity children are asked to act out a strength or positive component of another person. First, children think of a person they really admire, and then identify a specific quality that they like in that person. It can be somebody they know or someone they have seen who is really nice or good at something. Make sure they identify a positive role model who channels his or her abilities in a positive direction rather than someone who is good at destroying others. Once the children have clearly identified one good thing that this positive person does, they are ready to play the game. The goal of the game is for each child to pretend, make-believe or act as if he is this chosen person, for example, in the way he stands, walks, talks, thinks, feels, moves, plays, acts or interacts. In short, the child thinks about what it is that this person does that he likes, and then tries to act, feel or be like this person in some way for at least a certain period of time.

Some children act out the good parts of other people so well, and feel so good pretending to be them, that it becomes a positive part of their own behavior. "Acting as if you are" can help children become more considerate, helpful, strong, confident or calm. It can help children execute performance skills in a more competent, powerful or fluid way. Young children also enjoy playing this game by acting out the good parts of favorite animals.

Taking a Positive Step

There are many things that children are capable of doing that they think they are incapable of doing. This can result in refusing to even try things or pursue goals that are both beneficial and fully within reach. A simple example occurred while a 4-year-old boy was visiting with my family at a lake. The step from the shore to the dock on the edge of the lake was a long step for this child, but certainly within his capability. When we walked down towards the dock, he immediately said in a whining tone, "I can't do it!" He clung to this belief even though other children successfully made the "giant step." I took his hand in mine and offered to help him make the jump. He still refused to try. Finally I asked him to repeat out loud three times, "I can do it!, I can do it!, I can do it!" and to then immediately "step." He did exactly what I requested, leapt into the air and reached the dock with no problem. A huge smile covered his entire being. I applauded his step, "See Robbie, you can do it; you can do lots of things when you decide that you can do them."

When children think to themselves that they *can* do something, doubts are often suspended, at least momentarily. Then once they take a successful step, their experience reinforces the fact that they are capable. Taking a positive step physically is preceded and followed by taking a positive step mentally.

Echo Lake

This activity helps give children a vocabulary to strengthen their belief in themselves and their capabilities. The following script guides them into repeating a series of positive statements about themselves, which brings children a step closer to believing positive things about themselves.

Lie down and stretch yourself out in a comfortable position. Let yourself relax. Breathe easily and slowly. Breathe in slowly; feel the cool air move into your body. Breathe out slowly; feel the warm air leave your body. Breathe in slowly; feel the cool air. Breathe out slowly; feel the warm air. Good.

Now I want you to just listen to my voice. We're going to play a game called echoes. I will be the voice and you will be the echo.

Whatever you hear me say, you say out loud after me, just like an echo.

I am relaxed
I am breathing easy
I feel good
I like me
I do lots of good things
I am strong
I am healthy
I learn things quickly
I am smart
I am the boss of my body
If I talk to my body it will do what I say
I like to try new things
I know I can do many good things if I try
I feel good today
I am special
I am a good person
I am a good echoer
My echoes are now inside me
Today I feel strong and happy
I will enjoy this day

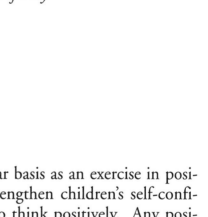

ECHO LAKE

Repeat "Echo Lake" on a regular basis as an exercise in positive thinking. The goal is to strengthen children's self-confidence and enhance their ability to think positively. Any positive statement can be included as a part of "Echo Lake" (e.g., I listen well, I like to help others, I look at the positive side of things, I am good at focusing, I am capable of doing many things very well, I have lots of good qualities).

Thinking in Ways That Help

Children need a vocabulary for positive thinking to begin to think more positively. This activity is designed to highlight the importance of positive thinking. It helps children to recognize the difference between positive and negative thinking and stimulates them to focus in positive ways. Begin by asking the children to think of some positive things ("good things") they can say to themselves to make themselves feel good and confident, for example before they try something new, do something important, go some place different, talk in front of the class, take a test, play a game, go into a race or competition or need a little lift.

Some examples of "good things" or helpful things they can say to themselves include:

I feel good, I feel very good, I feel super good, This will be fun, I can do this, I know I can do this, I'm going to make the best of this, I'll do (or try) my best, I'll try my hardest, I'm ready for this, I've done it before, I am prepared to do this, I'm looking forward to this, I want to do this, I love doing this, I am good at this, I'm smart enough, I'm good enough, I am strong, I am capable, I am confident in myself, I can see in my mind that I'm doing it great, I think I CAN—I think I CAN—I know I CAN, I can do anything, I am a good person, People like me, No matter what happens people who are important to me will still love me, No one is going to shoot me if I don't do it perfectly, The only thing that's important is to try my best—nothing else matters; I know how to do this—just focus on doing it, Come on you can do it, just go!

Some examples of not-so-good or hurtful things children may say to themselves include:

I can't do it, It's impossible, I'll probably be lousy, I'm no good, I might screw up, I won't be any good, People will laugh at me, People won't like me, What if I fail?, What if I can't do it?, I will disappoint people, I'll hate it, I won't like it, I won't do well, Everybody will be better than me, I'll blow it.

After the children are familiar with a few specific examples of positive and negative thoughts, ask them to list their own good thoughts (which are supportive and helpful) and not-so-good thoughts (which are negative, worrisome or hurtful). Write out their positive and negative thoughts in two separate columns on a chalk board or on a large piece of paper. Post their best positive thoughts in a prominent place and allow the children to add to the list whenever they discover new positive thoughts or different ways of expressing them.

It is interesting how easy it is for most children to come up with a long list of negative thoughts and how difficult it is for some children to think of positive thoughts. When asked to think of positive things to say to themselves, some children come up blank. However, they can always think of negative things or reasons why they won't like something or won't do well. One way to help children develop more positive options for constructive thinking is to provide them with specific positive examples. Another possibility is to take their list of negative thoughts and ask them to turn each of these negative thoughts into a positive thought by thinking the opposite. For example, change "This is boring" to "This is fun"; "I can't do it" to "I can do it"; "I'm not good" to "I am good"; "I won't like it" to "I will like it, let's give it a try." This has been a very effective exercise.

Point out that good thoughts help them feel confident, good about themselves, capable and ready: Good thoughts make you feel better, perform better and enjoy things more. Negative thoughts make you feel worse and perform worse. In short, good thoughts help you do the things you are capable of doing and accomplish the things you want to accomplish while negative thoughts do the opposite. So why not think good thoughts and say positive things to yourself and to others?

Ask the children to record their own list of best thoughts in their Highlight Book. This list of best thoughts can come from their own experience as well as from the best positive thoughts of others. Personal lists should include those thoughts that individual children feel are most positive and most relevant for them. To give children practice at positive thinking, ask them to read over their list of positive thoughts to themselves several times. Then ask them to read it out loud in a strong voice either alone or in a group. In a group setting this can be done one by one, or everyone can read their own list out loud at the same time. In either case children should read out their good thoughts with strength and conviction.

The goal of this exercise is to help children learn to listen to their own voice—their own best voice. They can listen to their own best voice by saying good things out loud, or by just thinking good things. Ask the children to think of a positive thought whenever they try something new, face an important challenge, catch themselves thinking a not-so-good thought or need a little lift. If ever you catch them slipping into a negative frame of mind, remind them to replace the negative thought with a positive thought.

"Thinking in ways that help" was introduced to a group of 6- to 9-year-old children in a day camp setting. Some of these children had grown accustomed to complaining, whining or finding something negative in almost everything. On this particular day the first thing we did was this exercise in positive thinking. After identifying positive and negative ways of thinking, the children were challenged to think in positive ways for the rest of the morning. For the rest of the day, most children were extremely positive and, when someone did make a negative comment, another child would say "Hey, that's negative thinking—replace it with a positive thought." This was an excellent beginning, however without reminders many will fall back into more familiar negative ways of thinking. It is important to repeat exercises like this and give plenty of positive reminders until positive thinking becomes a more natural way of being.

Being Positive with Others

Children's overall positiveness and self-confidence is directly influenced by the extent to which they are treated in positive ways by parents, teachers, coaches and other children. This activity is designed to increase children's overall positiveness experienced in school, at camp, in sport, and among family members at home.

Children are asked to respond to the following two questions (with reference to other kids, family members, teammates, teachers, coaches or parents):

1. What are some things that other kids (or teammates, teachers, coaches, parents) say or do that make you feel good?

2. What are some things that they say or do that make you feel bad?

Good things other kids do might include: ask me to play with them, play with me, be nice to me, say something nice to me. Bad things might include: call me names, laugh at me, fight, tell me I'm no good, say I can't play.

List the things that make the children feel good on a large piece of paper and post it on the wall. Discuss the "feel good" things with the children and explain to them that if everyone does more of those feel-good things and less of the feel-bad things, everyone will feel better and have more fun. Set a group goal for treating each other in positive ways. Encourage children to directly share how they feel when another child does something positive (e.g., "Thanks, that makes me feel really good") as well as when someone does something negative ("That wasn't very nice on my feelings; it makes me feel bad. It would be a lot better if you did something positive").

Targeting Positive Thoughts

One way to increase the frequency of positive behavior and decrease negative behavior is to challenge children, as well as yourself, to think and act only in positive ways for specified periods of time. For example, see if you can think only positive thoughts or say only positive things (nothing negative) for the next 2 minutes, 5 minutes, 10 minutes, etc. Gradually increase the length of time focused on the positive side. Also target specific circumstances in which to think and act only in positive ways—for example, when getting up in the morning; when interacting with family members; at recess; on rainy days; when trying something new; when playing games; before tests or competitions; when experiencing worries, self-doubts or setbacks.

Positive Flash Cards

This activity is designed to remind children to think and act in positive ways. In small groups each child writes or draws one positive reminder, happy thought or happy symbol on one card. When everyone has completed one card, each group silently flashes their cards for 10-15 seconds so that members of other groups can see them briefly but clearly.

The flashing of cards occurs as follows:

Group 1, please—each person in group 1 raises his/her card at the same time so other groups can see it. Group 2, please—each person in each group 2 raises his/her card at the same time, and so on until all cards have been raised.

Children in each group are challenged to look closely at the cards flashed by all the other groups so that they can remember as many positive sayings/symbols as possible, without writing anything down. Once all groups have finished flashing their cards, the children in each small group write down as many of the positive reminders as they can collectively remember. Each group then posts their original reminder cards and other groups see how close they came to remembering the original reminders.

Eight Key Reminders for Excelling at Living

When learning to think, act and love in more positive ways the following reminders are very important for all of us. Present these principles in simple ways and repeat them very often so the ideas really "sink in."

Only positive thoughts—Only positive thoughts help you to improve and help you do the good things you are capable of doing. So talk to yourself and to others only in ways that help you feel good and help you achieve your goals.

Only positive images—Only positive images of the things you want to accomplish help you to accomplish them. So imagine yourself doing the good things you really want to do, exactly the way you would like to do them—with joy, precision and total confidence.

Always focused—Only when you are fully focused on *doing* what you want to do, can you live and perform to your potential. So stay focused on the little things that free you to live joyfully and perform well. Focus only on the step in front on you. This will give you your best chance of living fully and performing to your true capacity.

Always I can—There is no advantage in approaching learning or performance situations thinking "I can't" or "maybe I'll mess it up." So approach every learning and performance opportunity thinking only "I CAN." Repeat "I CAN" to yourself and ACT like you can, even if you are not really sure you can. This will give you your best chance of achieving your goals and your dreams.

Always we can—When going after goals with friends, partners, family members or teammates, there is no advantage in thinking "we can't." So commit yourselves to enter these situations thinking and believing "WE CAN." We can always be positive and focus in ways that help us to be our best. This gives us our best shot at being successful and reaching our "team" goals. So act like you know WE CAN even if you are not totally sure, and focus on doing what will allow us to enjoy ourselves and perform well.

Always opportunities—There are opportunities in everything you see and do to learn, to grow, to develop, to expand, to stretch limits, to see openings, to find something good, to know yourself, to understand others, to overcome challenges, to become stronger, wiser, more balanced, more accomplished, more consistent, more compassionate and more human. So look for positive opportunities in everything you see and do. Find something magic, see the openings, live the highlights and seek out the possibilities for personal growth in everything.

Always lessons—In learning, performing and personal growth there are no errors, there are only lessons. So stay positive with yourself no matter what happens. Be sure to look for the good things you have done, draw out the positive lessons and act on those lessons so you continue to grow and improve.

Always supporting others—There is no advantage in putting down family members, classmates, friends or teammates and lots of advantages in supporting them. So be positive with others, look for their good points and support them wherever possible. This gives everyone the best chance of feeling good, improving, enjoying each other and being successful. ❤

2

Freeing Children from Stress

Stress is a very bad feeling that happens when you are mad, worried or sad. (8-year-old)

It feels like you have a big volcano inside you and it is going to burst. (12-year-old)

It's like a rubber band that is pulled to the very end and it's ready to snap. (10-year-old)

Your stomach feels really weird, like a gerbil running around inside your stomach. (11-year-old)

When my heart has tears. (7-year-old)

STRESS is like when . . .
>*You're lost in a big place*
>*You're playing marbles and you always lose*
>*You go out for pizza and it's not open*
>*You come home to nobody*
>*You feel all squeezed up*
>*You feel pulled apart*
>*You hurt inside*
>*You feel like you'll do everything wrong*
>*You have lots to do and don't know what to do about it*

You have 1000 things to do and only 12 minutes to do it
You feel confused, sad, mad, uptight, guilty, worried, scared,
tense or pressured
Your stomach turns into a knot
You want to bite your nails or cry
You feel like throwing up

Something stressful just happened to me. I can't find my
2 cookies in my lunch. (5-year-old)

As a parent or teacher, you can protect children from a certain amount of negative stress, especially in the early years, but sooner or later they will need to learn how to cope with stressful situations on their own—these situations will be beyond your control. You have two basic choices here. You can hope that your children learn effective focusing and coping strategies on their own, or you can begin to teach them these skills. The risk with hoping they will learn on their own is that many children left to their own devices grow into adults who suffer unnecessarily from high levels of stress. Most children *do not* learn effective strategies for relaxation and coping with stress, on their own.

You can help your children learn to focus effectively and deal with their emotions in healthy ways right now, by introducing them to the following concepts and activities. By doing so, you will help them develop important stress control skills that they will carry with them for life.

Children are exposed to many potentially stressful situations as they attempt to understand and adapt to the changing world around them. Potential sources of stress come from people and events in their immediate environment; adult expectations; family conflicts; parental absence; peer expectations; the demands of schools, teachers and coaches to learn and perform; the desire to "fit in," be accepted or "perfect" in various endeavors. As children attempt to meet and adapt to the many expectations, roles and demands placed upon them by adults and peers, they come face-to-face with uncertainty, fear and stress. The earlier you begin to teach children effective ways of dealing with the various stresses they face, the better off they will be and you will be.

Children's worries about many things serve no useful purpose, and their worries often lead to negative psychological and physiological consequences. They may worry about making errors, failing to please, having to perform, being late, forgetting something, being judged, fitting in, not being accepted or loved, receiving medical treatment (if they are sick), getting needles or going to the dentist. They worry about the possibility of being left out, yelled at, put down or rejected by parents, teachers, brothers, sisters, other children, instructors or coaches. They may soak in their anxiety about doing something "wrong," losing a game or falling short of someone's expectations, long after it can possibly serve any productive purpose. Teaching children simple stress control strategies is an effective way of helping them to avoid or lighten up on this kind of unhealthy anxiety.

Sources of Children's Stress

Our studies have shown that all children experience some stress, most within the following six domains. "People" stress is by far the greatest source of stress for children, followed by school stress and sport/activity/performance stress.

People stress—revolves around conflict, arguments, feelings of rejection or guilt primarily with respect to parents, teachers, friends, siblings or other children.

Parents/Teachers

my mom got mad at me
my dad yelled at me
my teacher was not nice

Friends

my friend was bugging me
my friend likes my other friend more than me

Siblings

I was in a fight with my sister
I wasn't getting enough attention because there is a new baby

Other children

bullies
I got teased by dumb boys
somebody kicked me

School stress—revolves around homework, tests and meeting school-related expectations.

I felt nervous before the test
I was worried after the test
I was not finished my homework
I presented my speech

Performance/sport/activity stress—revolves around pre-performance anxiety, failing to win, pass or meet expectations.

I am afraid I won't do good
I did not pass my test
we lost the game
I got 0 points

Loss of control—revolves around frustration, loss, a sense of helplessness, or fear.

> *waiting for an answer*
> *I could not do what I wanted to do*
> *I lost my dog*
> *I am afraid of the dark*

Sickness/illness/injury—revolves around stress related to being injured, getting sick or receiving medical treatment.

> *I was sick*
> *I hurt myself*
> *I had to go to the doctor's office*

Sleeping problems—revolves around not being able to sleep, scary thoughts or bad dreams.

> *I could not get to sleep*
> *I had a bad nightmare that was scary*

Children who were taught the Feeling Great relaxation and stress control activities successfully applied them in stressful situations within all six of these domains. The strategies they learned helped them: to *relax* ("to get to sleep at night." "to relax my muscles," "to relax when I am stressed out," "to lower my heart rate"), to *avoid stress* ("to keep calm so that I don't get upset," "to solve problems," "to put my worries behind me instead of keeping them inside," "there are always lessons and no mistakes"), to *deal with stress* ("to get stress away," "to control stress," "to not be scared," "to calm down when things are bothering me"), to *focus* ("to focus on good things," "to listen to others better," "to concentrate better for tests and for sports") and to *feel better* ("to ease my mind," "to feel better," to feel fresh," "to encourage me," "to feel happier," "to be a better person").

The Problem with Stress

In some of the original experiments on the detrimental effects of stress, researchers tied down healthy white rats by their paws for a predetermined period of one to two days. Within 30 hours all of those rats were dead. They literally killed themselves due to their state of alarm and the related bio-chemical reactions within their own bodies. An analysis of their inner organs revealed that the stressful experience had resulted in numerous deep bleeding ulcers in their stomachs, a marked enlargement of their adrenal cortex and an intense shrinkage of the thymus and lymph nodes. As a result of becoming stressed and maintaining a state of alarm, they subjected their bodies to biochemical agents so damaging that continuous exposure to it resulted in death within hours or days (Selye, 1956, 1974).

My first thought upon reading about these experiments was that if someone could have simply communicated with these rats and said, "Just settle back and relax—you'll be out of here by the morning," they would not have suffered any serious effects from the experience. Unfortunately, they did not have any effective stress control strategies available to them. That's why their stressful reactions literally ate their insides away.

It is not the "stressful" event itself that is so important, but rather how you react to it. Your reaction to potentially stressful events that occur over the course of your day or week is what impacts most on your well-being. The same is true for children.

A little stress, or even a lot now and then, is not going to kill you. Stress is a part of life, a part of living. However, a continuous diet of stress, in the absence of good coping skills, will affect your mental and physical health, your relationships and the quality of your life. Stress heightens irritability and increases your susceptibility to various kinds of illness. It lowers your resistance, weakens your immune system and prolongs recovery from mental and physical setbacks.

Your body undergoes specific biochemical reactions in response to stress, which affects your general disposition, your psychological well-being, your capacity to concentrate and your ability to enjoy simple things. Stressful experiences often leave you feeling tired, exhausted or sick. In long-term situations, negative stress can destroy your immune system and your entire state of health. You place yourself at risk of dying spiritually, emotionally or physically, long before you have to. High levels of stress can be withstood for just so long. Sooner or later people who live highly stressful, unbalanced lives become victims of the constant wear and tear associated with stress, and their families may also become victims.

Children who acquire effective stress control skills will be protected from the negative consequences experienced by the little white rats and by human adults suffering from stress-related illnesses because they will have learned more positive ways of coping. There will be little chance of these children eating away their own insides in response to potentially stressful situations that are not really that important or over which they have no direct control.

Carrying a Healthy Perspective

The attitude you carry into various potentially stressful situations directly affects how much stress you experience, how long things bother you, how much your mental and physical health suffers and how you influence those around you.

I am reminded of the time that little Melanie's mother was driving Melanie to her kindergarten. Her dad usually drove her to school on his way to work at a frantic pace, darting from one lane to another, fuming at anyone or anything in his path. This morning Melanie's mother took over. As Mom calmly drove through the morning traffic, Melanie peered out the window at the other cars. Then with a perplexed look on her face she turned to her mom and asked, "Where are all the bastards today? Where are all the bastards?" Her mom paused for a moment of silent reflection and then replied, "They only come out when Daddy's driving."

Different perspectives, or choosing to view the world in a different way, allows us to react to the same situation differently, both emotionally and physically.

To ensure your children experience less stress, you can do two important things. First, you can help your children develop a positive outlook and balanced perspective which they carry into the various situations they face, so that they experience more joy, more personal control and less stress. Second, you can help them learn simple but effective methods for dealing with the stress they do experience, so that it does not become too extreme or linger too long.

The primary objectives of placing stress control strategies in the hands and minds of children is to enhance their personal well-being by helping them avoid unnecessary stress and by preventing them from soaking too long in emotions that are self-destructive or destructive towards others. Effective mental skills not only ease anxiety but lead to a more constructive focus. This frees children to feel and grow as human beings without becoming paralyzed in the process.

The most important first step in helping children to carry a more positive and less stressful perspective is to ensure that they feel your love, acceptance and respect. This will allow them to believe in themselves and to recognize that their basic human worth remains, regardless of how they perform or what happens to them on a given day. Do everything in your power to assure your children, and to demonstrate to them, that their intrinsic value remains intact even though they may make an error, fall short of an expectation or mess something up. Listen attentively to their feelings. Respect their concerns. Encourage them to feel their emotions and share their feelings. This is an important part of helping them become fully human.

The things that worry children are often small things that they view as very big. Most of their worries are related to feelings about their own fragility or concerns about acceptance. By acknowledging a child's feelings, you accept that child as an important, valued person, and as a distinct human entity. Once you have done this, it is easier for the child to view things from a more balanced perspective. In situations where children experience big worries over seemingly little things, first accept their feelings, and then point out that sometimes the things we worry about do not turn out to be as important as we first think they are. This is also a good time to remind children that you and others who really care about them will always continue to love and accept them, and that all their good qualities will remain regardless of how this turns out. When children's worries are related to something big, show your empathy for their concerns, accept their feelings, share your love and try to help them realize that their concerns are normal.

The second step in helping children live a more balanced and healthy perspective is to teach them mental skills that will enable them to let go of unnecessary worries, particularly when those worries are centered around events that are beyond their immediate control. It is important to help children understand that there are things they can control and things they cannot control. Worrying in itself is not likely to change the things that are beyond their control. One thing we know for certain is that children cannot change the results of an event that has already passed, no matter how hard they try or how much stress they allow themselves to experience over it.

While you continue to encourage children to pursue their dreams, you must also help them learn to avoid unnecessary or prolonged stress over events that are either totally beyond their control or not worth the emotional energy. Helping children to think in more positive ways is particularly beneficial when anxiety lingers on long after it can possibly serve any useful purpose. The major challenge here is to teach children to prepare for new experiences and draw lessons from past experiences without dwelling on the negative. This process involves teaching children to think positively, look for good things, focus on controlling what is within their potential control and keep things in perspective. By empowering children with positive mental skills and healthy perspectives, you free them to spend less time and energy worrying, and more time engaged in positive, uplifting pursuits.   ❤

3

Teaching Children Stress-Free Perspectives

What's the difference between stress and relaxation?

Stress is like something is bottled up inside. Relaxation is like opening the bottle and letting all the tension pour out. (10-year-old)

Stress is like I'm in a maze of frustration. Relaxation is like a pair of hands that lift you out of the maze. (9-year-old)

Stress is like winding yourself up. Relaxation is like letting yourself unwind. (8-year-old)

When you're stressed you're in a rush. When you're relaxed you're all slowed down. (7-year-old)

Stress makes you feel bad and relaxing makes you feel good. (8-year-old)

There are a variety of approaches from which you can choose to help children learn to carry more positive, less stressful perspectives. All of the activities presented in this chapter have been effective in helping children to free themselves from stress in potentially stressful situations. They provide a simple, understandable framework for stress control that children easily relate to. Start by selecting a couple of activities that you feel are most likely to work with your children. Let the children try them and decide on their own which they like best.

"Can't Do Magic"

While working with 5-year-old pre-school children, I tried to explain the concept of not worrying about what is beyond our control. On one occasion a little girl had just spilled a jar of yellow paint and was clearly feeling quite upset about it. I said to her and the other children: "It's okay that the paint got spilled. Sometimes things like that happen to all of us. It doesn't help us to worry about it because it's already done. Worrying won't make the paint jump back into the jar. So let's not worry about it, let's just help each other clean it up, and maybe we can learn a lesson for next time about how we can help the paint stay in the jar."

The children looked at me with those beautiful wide-open eyes, and the little girl who spilled the paint was relieved by my words of acceptance. I wasn't really sure if my message had gotten through for future use, but I was hopeful that it had.

Later that same day we went outside and hiked to a nearby pond to observe clusters of frogs' eggs and other forms of aquatic life. To get a closer view, one of the little boys walked along a fallen log on the edge of the shallow pond. Before long he slipped off the log into the water, soaking his shoes and socks. His eyes darted up with a sheepish look, as he glanced over to see if the teacher had noticed. At almost the same instant, one of the little girls blurted out, "Oh look, Alex got his feet wet." She hesitated for a second, and then continued by saying, "Oh, but it doesn't matter because it's already did, and we can't do magic."

She pointed out his predicament, but also reminded him,

and the rest of us, to keep things in perspective. Drawing upon the image of "magic" to clarify the concept of being unable to control the past was totally her own creation. I had never mentioned the word magic. She told us in her own language ("We can't do magic") what I had tried to explain to her in my language. We cannot control the past, so why worry in vain about something we cannot do anything about? Her comments seemed to calm Alex and he breathed a sigh of relief. Most exciting for me was that my message had gotten through.

Children have acted upon her "can't do magic" concept in a variety of situations. When a 4-year-old accidentally knocked over a glass of milk at lunch, a 5-year-old quickly piped up and said, "It doesn't matter 'cause we can't do magic," and got a cloth to clean it up. I reinforced this perspective by saying, "Yup, we can't do magic and make the milk jump back into the glass. It's no big deal. We just have to wipe it up and learn a lesson for next time." I felt good about that and so did the children.

When a child spills a glass of milk, knocks over a plant or loses a game, it is over and done. She "can't do magic" and control the past, so we are best to pick up the pieces, pull out the lessons, set it aside and move on without unnecessarily upsetting them or ourselves. We can draw upon this "magic" concept in many situations which arise with children. It empowers children to experience less unnecessary stress and helps them learn to draw lessons from experiences without needlessly torturing themselves.

Umbala Kiki

I have gained some important insights about living in harmony with ourselves, others and our environment by studying the lifestyles of aboriginal people.

One of the lessons I learned about helping children remove negative stress emerged while I was living in a remote village in the jungles of Papua New Guinea. I noticed that at the conclusion of children's competitive games, all the children came together in a huddle (or circle) and one player gently touched every other player on the shoulder, one by one. As she touched each player she said, "Umbala kiki, umbala kiki". She then walked over and placed her hand on a nearby tree, and put "it" into the tree. "It" turned out to be any bad feelings, anxiety or animosity that may have surfaced in the game. This was a simple, effective way to put the game away. They simply left "it" in the tree. The village elders told me that this tradition was introduced many centuries ago to ensure that people continued to live happily with each other and within themselves. The physical act of removing anxiety and putting "it" in the tree helped to ensure that no one left the game in a negative frame of mind. Anxiety, negative thoughts or animosity that may have otherwise lingered on after the game were thereby laid to rest.

Umbala Kiki (children's script)

I once lived in a little jungle village in a country called Papau New Guinea. The people lived in little huts made from trees and leaves. They had no electricity, or TVs or stoves or bathtubs. The weather was warm all the time and there were lots of fruit trees and gardens and birds and rivers and streams. The people were very nice and friendly and the children loved to play together outside. They laughed a lot and had lots of fun playing.

I noticed that when they finished playing games all the children on both teams got together in a circle. One of the children gently touched every other child on the arm or the shoulder, one by one and said, "umbala kiki, umbala kiki" which means I take it from you, I take it from you. She then placed her hand on a nearby tree. The reason she did this was to take away any unhappy feelings, worries, or anger that may have come up during the game. This was a good way of taking away bad feelings, just in case any of the children were feeling bad. They called it "treeing it." The village chief, who was 110 years old, told me that his people have been doing this for many, many years. He told me that "treeing" unhappy thoughts helps people to continue to live happily with each other and within themselves.

You can use "tree it" in lots of good ways too. If ever you are feeling worried or upset about something—in a game or at home or in school—walk over to a tree or wall or desk and "tree it." As you touch the wall or desk or tree, imagine yourself putting all your worries, or tension or unhappy feelings in the tree or wall. Then turn around and smile, knowing that you have let your worries go and you are free to be positive and happy.

Physically going through the actions of touching a child, removing the anxiety, walking to a tree, touching the tree and putting "it" in the tree increases the chances of the children actually leaving those feelings behind. This is an effective way of teaching children to shift focus and it helps them learn at an early age that it is possible to get rid of unwanted or harmful anxiety.

When first sharing this approach with your children, walk them through the process. First, explain the "tree it" concept in the simplest terms. Then take them through each step, much the same as occurred with the village children. Touch the child gently, say I'm taking "it" (i.e., those worries) from you. Then walk with the child to the tree (or rock, or blackboard, or wall) and say "we are putting all those worries or bad feelings in here" as you firmly touch the tree or rock. "There, now they're in the tree." Give each child a turn at "treeing it."

Since first discovering this concept children have used it in all kinds of situations to avoid dwelling on hassles, distractions, worries, self-doubts or self put-downs. Children have "treed," suspended or put away their unwanted stress or negative thoughts in walls, water, rocks, desks, tables, floors, boxes, jars, pots, bags, lockers, shelves, benches and boards around rinks. Some have poured their worries down drains, flushed them down toilets or washed them away while swimming or showering. Others have removed negative stress or tension by letting it flow out of themselves into a warm bath or out an open window. One child chose to put his worry in a rock and threw the rock into a lake. A young figure skater decided to put her pre-competition anxiety into a jar before going out to skate. She half filled the jar with water, symbolically poured in her worries and negative thoughts, added soap, sealed the jar, and shook it to wash away her worries. Then she went out on the ice and skated a worry-free program.

The "tree it" concept has also been useful in helping children put away worries that are interfering with their sleep. For example, on one occasion my child was lying in bed worrying about having left a homework book at school. Our conversation unfolded in the following way:

Child: The teacher will be really mad; she'll say forgetting is no excuse.

T.O.:   It's too bad your book is at school, but we all forget things sometimes. There's nothing we can do to get the book here right now, and worrying won't help.

Child: But I can't help it.

T.O.:   You can help your worry go away. It's your

worry. Put it in the wall and leave it there.

Child: I can't reach the wall. (She was lying in bed a couple of feet from the wall.)

T.O.:   Then give it to me and I'll put it in the wall.

Child: No, then you'll have it!

She leaned over, put her hand on the wall, and the worry was gone. I gently took her hand in mine, began massaging between her thumb and index finger and said to her, "This is an old Chinese trick for sleeping." We both laughed. Shortly after she drifted off to sleep—worry free.

While working with our national ski team in the Andes Mountains I discovered a Chilean ski instructor who used a similar approach to help children put away their fear before skiing down a hill. At the top of the hill she dug a little hole in the snow, asked the child to put his fear in the hole and then refilled the hole with snow. Now that his fear was temporarily frozen, she asked him to think only of what he had to do to ski well. It was an effective means of helping the child to "freeze" or suspend his worries long enough to refocus his attention on skiing, as opposed to worrying. The same approach can be applied in other settings as well, for example, by digging a hole in the sand or earth.

In Guatemala, children were encouraged to place their worries in the hands of tiny dolls before going to bed, so they would have a good night's sleep. The dolls were then placed under their pillow or in a tiny wooden box for the night. This practice was introduced as a way of helping young children learn to put away their worries. The children were told that the little wooden dolls (the size of match sticks) could do all the worrying for them, and that their worries wouldn't hurt the wooden dolls.

Wooden matches, toothpicks or small stones can be substituted for tiny dolls. For example, a child can place one unwanted worry, fear or negative thought into each match stick or toothpick, place it in a small match box, and close it whenever he wants to set aside that worry or negative thought.

At the highest performance levels, "tree it" has also been effective. Alwyn Morris, an Olympic paddler with whom I worked for a number of years, was dwelling on a disappointing performance after his first event at the Olympic Games. He was having difficulty putting away the first event, but it was important that he do so because he still had a remaining event in which to compete. He went to the swimming pool, pushed down to the bottom, let all his air out and left his disappointment about the first race on the bottom of the pool. In his own words, he decided to "pool it." It was at that point that he shifted focus. He returned to the race course in a positive frame of mind, experienced a personal best performance and won the race.

The term "park it," a modern version of "tree it," has become a well-known and useful term for many athletes in pursuit of excellence. On one occasion a basketball player had been "parking" quite a few hassles in a row: officials' "bad calls," opponents' harassment and missed shots. After another "unjust" call by the official, the athlete began to react, and his coach yelled, "park it!" The player responded, "My lot's getting full, coach." Sometimes our lots do begin to fill up. That is usually when we need a breather, a break or a little time-out for ourselves to clear our minds and put things back in perspective.

Changing Channels

Changing mental channels is an effective means of helping children learn to control their own focus and anxiety. The idea came to me as a result of observing children watch television.

I've noticed two things in this regard. First, children are totally capable of fully focusing on things that interest them. I'm sure a house could literally fall down around some children and it would go unnoticed because they are so completely riveted to what they are watching. The second thing I noticed is the extent to which children are capable of instantly refocusing. A tearful child who has hurt herself, or a child howling with discontent, is capable of immediately shifting focus when a favorite cartoon is turned on the television. They can instantly stop crying and forget about the hurt or incident that precipitated their distress. Children can absorb themselves in one program or activity and then almost immediately absorb themselves in another.

Most children in technological societies have experienced changing channels on a television set and have witnessed a concrete result. For example, they can literally click through different channels to find what they want, or change channels if what they are watching is scary, upsetting or worrisome. They simply switch the channel away from the worry to something better or more appropriate for them. This same concept of "changing channels" can be used to teach children to change mental channels.

The remote control switch that accompanies most televisions can be put to good use with children when explaining the idea of changing mental channels. Wooden or Styrofoam replicas of channel changers also work well. Present the idea of "changing channels" to children as a game that is played in the following way:

Changing Channels (script for children)

Get yourself into a comfortable position. Let yourself relax. Breathe easily and slowly. Close your eyes and just listen to my voice.

In some ways you are like a TV set. You have lots of different channels inside your head—happy channels, sad channels, worry channels, scary channels, fuzzy channels, funny channels, focused channels, good (positive) channels, bad (negative) channels, tense channels and relaxed channels. All of these channels are inside your head. The great thing about being a person and not a TV set is that you can decide which channel you want to be on today. You have a remote control switch inside you. If you are on a channel that makes you worried, and you don't feel like being worried, you can switch channels by thinking about something positive, good, happy, relaxed, fun or funny. If you are on a grumpy (or negative) channel and would prefer to be on a happy (or positive) channel, you can switch channels by thinking about a highlight or by doing something happy or positive.

When first trying to change channels you can actually push the button on the remote control channel changer as you try to switch channels in your own mind. Later on you can change channels by imagining that the remote control switch is in your hand. Press your thumb against your first finger as you try to change channels in your mind. You can get really good at changing channels by practicing every day. Imagine that the control switch is inside your head so you can change channels or shift focus anytime you want to just by thinking about something relaxing or positive.

When this activity is first introduced, encourage children to actually push the button on the remote control channel changer as they try to switch channels in their own minds. Later on, encourage them to change channels by imagining that the remote control switch is in their hand. Ask them to press their thumb against their first finger as they attempt to change channels. Finally, encourage children to imagine that the control switch is inside their head so they can change channels or shift focus any time they want to by just thinking about something constructive.

Channel Changers

Once the children have been introduced to the concept of changing channels, let them make their own channel changers. Provide the children with empty egg cartons, cardboard, construction paper, or small blocks made of wood or Styrofoam, along with crayons, pencils, magic markers and scissors. Suggest some channels they can put on their channel changer (e.g. a happy channel, sad channel, funny channel, focused channel, positive channel, negative channel, angry channel, relaxed channel), and let them add their own channels. Once the channel changers are completed let the children show and tell about their channels.

Children can also use their homemade channel changers to play some games. Either you or one of your children can call out changes in channels that are on his or her channel changer. The children act out these changes, for example from sad to happy, stressed to relaxed, weak to strong, not confident to very confident, angry to calm, bored to focused, negative to positive, grumpy to laughing. Always end on a happy channel. Let the children create some of their own channel changing games.

Happy Channels

On one occasion a 6-year-old boy came for a sleep-over. Shortly after going to sleep he woke up and told me he had had a bad dream. He was dreaming about a "scary" movie he had seen a few days earlier. I asked him to try to change channels by recalling a very funny cartoon that we had seen earlier that day. He tried to imagine that scene and recalled how we had laughed and laughed. He began to smile. The scary channel faded and the happy channel took over. With that positive image in his mind he was able to sleep well throughout the night with no scary dreams.

On another occasion a pre-school sleepover guest was lying in bed thinking of monsters with yellow eyes that were trying to kill him. When I asked him to try to change the image into something friendly, he transformed his scary giant into a friendly giant turtle with polka dots on its belly. The turtle he created in his imagination was standing up on its back legs with one hand up in the air, and was giving out free ice cream cones—chocolate, pink and mint. The turtle had a big chocolate ice cream cone on top of its head with icing on top of it. The friendly giant walked over to the child and said, "The ice cream is free. What kind would you like?" The little boy took "chocolate with pink and chocolate icing." That laid to rest the scary yellow-eyed monster.

Another evening as I was tucking my daughter into bed she said, "I have scary things in my head." As it turned out she had watched a "scary" video at a friend's house earlier that day and those images were stuck in her head. I suggested that she try to think of something funny to chase away the scary images. She said, "like what?" I reminded her of a couple of funny scenes in a very humorous Charlie Chaplin film we had seen called *The Champion*. In one of the scenes, Charlie ends up in a boxing ring pitted against a big hulk. A small dog jumps into the ring and saves Charlie by clenching onto the back of the big hulk's shorts. She laughed as she recalled that scene. By tuning in to that "Charlie" channel she was able to quickly settle down and go to sleep.

The next night the scary images from the video returned. I went through the same scenario and reminded her of the little dog in the ring. She said, "We did that last night!" It seemed we needed a new image. I thought for a moment and said, "Remember when I tried to do a spin on the grass earlier today and ended up twirling into a heap on the ground?" When I actually did that unintended flop she thought it was hilarious. But instead of laughing she said, "Oh, I know a good one. At recess today there was a big kid who was trying to be so cool. He tried one of those twirling karate kicks and ended up flopping on the ground. It was really funny." With that image in her mind, she rolled over, closed her eyes and drifted off to sleep.

On subsequent occasions if anyone had trouble getting to sleep they would often ask, "What's a good image?" If they could not think of one, I would suggest one. Quiet images worked as well—for example, imagining that everything inside you is completely quiet just like when a lake is perfectly calm in the early morning mist.

Good Mood Channels

When I was at a friend's house for dinner, a 6-year-old boy was sad and weeping because he felt his older siblings and their friend had treated him unfairly. When the dinner was put on the table he remained crying on the floor in the darkened hallway. I went to him, listened to his feelings through his sobs and accepted his plight. He still refused to come and eat. He said he wasn't hungry and wasn't going to eat. I took off my watch, showed him how the stopwatch worked, set it on zero and said, "Why don't you feel bad for two more minutes and then come to the table for some great food when the stopwatch reaches two minutes." His attention was immediately absorbed on the watch, his sobs stopped almost instantly and exactly two minutes later he came to the table, proudly showed me two minutes on the timer, sat down and ate a huge and happy meal. He had changed channels by effectively shifting to another focus.

When I was visiting some relatives, I watched a parent yell at a child for hitting another child. Because I had been observing the children at play for some time, I knew his hit was unintentional. He was turning to get something and the other child just happened to run into his path, was hit and began to cry. Immediately after being screamed at, the child ran and hid in a little cranny next to his bed. I informed his mother that the hit had been unintentional. She called to him from the other room but he would not respond. I knew he was upset and stewing inside, which wasn't doing his health or his disposition any good. He wasn't ready to talk. So I sat on the bed across from where he was holed up, and silently batted a balloon in his direction. He batted it back, I batted it back to him and he batted it back to me. When I had to stretch my body off the bed and roll onto the floor to reach the balloon, he smiled and then laughed. He was fine from that point on. I was able to ease him out of his sulking and short-cut his anxiety by getting him to shift his focus to our playful interaction. If you can help children to shift focus away from their anxiety, or sulking, to something else which is very concrete and positive, in this case hitting a balloon back and forth, you are usually successful in helping them change channels.

Parents often help crying infants or very young children to change channels by holding them, rocking them, talking or singing to them, lifting them, rubbing them, moving them or giving them objects with which to play or chew on. When this works it is because the child shifts focus or awareness from something unpleasant to something else which is different, interesting, more pleasant or more absorbing. Parents essentially change channels for the infant by removing him from the stressful situation, by introducing him to a different activity or by guiding him into an alternate focus.

With young children you can guide a shift in channels by doing something with them that they like to do (playing, reading, walking, singing), or by saying something that creates a positive picture or an absorbing focus ("remember that baby horse we saw at the farm?," "next week we are going to visit Grandma—what do you want to do when we are there?," "look at this neat little leaf," "did you see this spider?"). However, ultimately children have to learn to change internal channels on their own. They have to gain control over their own ability to maintain a positive, meaningful focus, and, when they waver, to reorient their own focus in a positive direction. You can help children learn to do this by encouraging them to direct their thoughts, images and focus away from unproductive channels to more positive, productive channels.

The importance of shifting to a positive, concrete and absorbing focus holds true for other ages and domains as well. Members of the national basketball team with whom I worked for a number of years discovered that if they missed a shot or made an error in a game, they could reduce their anxiety, eliminate negative thinking and get right back into the game if they quickly refocused by changing channels. Normally what worked best was a quick reminder to shift focus away from negative thinking to a very concrete focus within the player's immediate control such as "move your feet," "get back" (on defense) or "find your man" (the player you are supposed to be guarding). This quick shift in focus prevented players from dwelling on the missed shot, error or disappointment, and put them back in control of what they were doing ("playing their game").

There are many ways to change channels: focus on something else, do something else, go someplace else, think something else, look at something else, listen to something else, imagine something else or put your worries somewhere else. Changing channels always involves a change in focus—from immersing yourself in one thing to immersing yourself in another.

The goal of changing mental channels is to put you back in control, on a positive path. This is accomplished by switching from a negative channel to a positive channel or from a worry channel to a beneficial channel, whenever a switch might be healthy or helpful. The channel to which you switch can be anything more positive or less worrisome that absorbs your interest, attention or focus in a positive way.

I have often used the following script with teenagers and youth to help get them on the right channel:

Get yourself into a comfortable position. Breathe easily and slowly and just listen to my voice.

It's amazing what you can do with yourself and your performance when you enter the right mental channel. Your brain has lots of different channels—positive channels, negative channels, stressful channels, relaxed channels, fun channels and focused channels. All of these channels are inside your head. You can decide which channel you want to be on, at different points during your day. You have the remote control switch within you. If you are on a stressful channel and you would prefer to be on a more relaxed channel, switch channels—by thinking of something uplifting, happy, funny, or by doing something relaxing. If you are on a negative channel and would prefer to be on a more positive channel, change channels—by saying something positive to yourself, by focusing on what is within your control, or by doing something constructive.

If you don't like the channel you are on, change channels. Think of how you would prefer to experience this moment, or live this day. Tune into a channel that helps you feel good about yourself, and helps you accomplish the things you want to accomplish. choose a confident channel, a channel that allows you to be positive and supportive with yourself and others. You can choose the channel, or change the channel, whenever you want, because the control switch lies within your own thinking.

Choose Positive Thoughts, Positive Images and Positive Lessons. See opportunities in everything. Believe in yourself and in what you are doing. Follow your own path. Choose the most positive channel you can imagine—the channel that makes you feel great.

Teaching children and youth to become proficient at changing channels is an excellent way to help them gain a greater sense of personal control over themselves and the situations they face. Positive channel changing helps them learn to focus on the positive, avoid magnifying the negative and rid themselves of prolonged or counter-productive anxiety. The key to self-directed channel changing lies in encouraging children to initiate a shift in focus from something negative and absorbing to something positive and absorbing, on their own. Everyone is capable of doing this. However, it takes persistent practice and lots of reminders. ❤

4

Relaxation

Relaxation is when you lie down and breathe slowly. Memories of bad stuff goes away. Your troubles disappear. You just feel calm and good—like you're free. (9-year-old)

Relaxation is when you let your whole body go loose and forget your worries. (10-year-old)

RELAXATION is like . . .
a bowlful of Jell-O
taking a suntan
lying in a hammock
getting a foot massage
when you're rubbery like spaghetti
when nothing bugs you
when you are really wiggly and about to fall asleep
when you are feeling nice and cozy and don't want to move
a place where you can drowsy down
not thinking of bad things
letting your mind drift away
letting out all the tension
enjoying a little happy thing
you're in a dream world like floating on a cloud

Relaxation is like a nice hide-out. It's like stretching out in the sun, feeling warm and relaxed and happy. (7-year-old)

The activities in the next four chapters are designed to help children improve their skills in relaxation, mental imagery, focusing and shifting focus. By developing these mental skills children will be better able to positively influence their own health, mood, performance and the direction of their lives. They will become increasingly aware that they have the capacity to control their own bodies, their own focus, their own stress and their own performance. They will also become more skillful at doing so.

Present the activities in a fun-filled and supportive manner. Allow children to develop positive mental skills within a milieu of sharing enjoyable moments together each day.

Activities to Relax

Children can relax in a variety of ways. The following activities, created to free children to enter a complete state of enjoyable relaxation, have been successful in helping young children learn to relax. These activities can be introduced virtually any time, anywhere: in a classroom, gym, park or living room, or before going to sleep at night. They can be presented to groups of children or individually to one child at a time. When presenting relaxation activities to groups of children it is nice if they each have their own little mat or blanket, or spread out a parachute on the floor or ground and let them each find a space. At home, children can relax on the rug, on a mattress or on their bed.

Before beginning relaxation exercises it is helpful to dim the lights and ask the children to close their eyes. Activities designed to elicit relaxed feelings or vivid imagery often work better initially when done with eyes closed. This gives children a better chance of closing off outside distractions so they can focus only on relaxing images, positive thoughts and the feelings associated with the activity.

Read the following relaxation scripts to the children or use our relaxation audio-tapes (see Resource section). Before beginning each of these exercises ask the children to sit or lie down in a comfortable position. If they are lying down ask them to stretch out their legs and to rest their arms quietly at their sides. Ensure that there is enough space between children so that they are not distracted by anyone else. If it is not feasible for the children to lie down, ask them to sit in a comfortable position with their heads resting in a relaxed position at their desks. Ask the children to focus *only* on listening to your voice or the voice on the audio-tape for the next few minutes.

The best medium for tuning out unwanted or disruptive distractions lies within children's internal focus. Encourage children to practice focusing so fully on the activity that external distractions or worries disappear naturally.

Spaghetti Toes

This activity is designed to give children practice at "thinking into" different body parts. It draws upon the image of cooked spaghetti to help children create and send a relaxing message to various muscles in their body. The first time you introduce this activity, start by giving each child a piece of uncooked spaghetti. Let the child examine it closely to see and feel how stiff it is, and how easily it breaks. Then give each child a piece of cooked spaghetti (warm, if possible). Let them examine it to see and feel how flexible it is and how easily it can curl up or wiggle without breaking. Point out that stiff, hard, tense spaghetti (uncooked) is fragile and breaks more easily than flexible, soft, relaxed spaghetti (cooked). People are a bit like that too. Young children like to actually watch the spaghetti cook and to eat a little bowl full before or after doing spaghetti toes.

Once you are ready to begin the exercise, read the following script to the children. With pre-school children you may want to shorten the script. To make things easier, record the script on tape or use our audio-tape entitled "Relaxation and Life Skills Activities for Children and Youth." All of the scripts in this book are available on audio-tape (see Resource section).

There are lots of games you can play with your body. We'll start with one called Spaghetti Toes. I wonder how good you are at talking to your toes. I'll bet you are pretty good. Let's find out.

Tell the toes on one of your feet to wiggle. Are they wiggling? On just one foot? Good! Now tell these toes to stop wiggling. Tell the toes on your other foot to wiggle. Tell them to wiggle real slow—and faster—and real slow again—slower—stop. Did your toes listen to you? Good.

If you talk to different parts of your body, like you just did with your toes, your body will listen to you . . . especially if you talk to it a lot. I'm going to show you how you can be the boss of your body by talking to it.

First I want to tell you something about spaghetti. I like spaghetti. I'll bet you do too. Did you ever see spaghetti before it's cooked? It's kind of cold and hard and stiff and it's easy to break. When it's cooked, it's warm and soft and it kinda lies down and curls up on your plate.

I want to see if you can talk to your toes to get them to go soft and warm and sleepy like spaghetti lying on your plate. You might have to talk to them quite a bit to make them know what you want them to do, but I know they can do it.

Wiggle your toes on one foot. Now tell these toes to stop wiggling. Tell them to go soft and sleepy like warm spaghetti lying on your plate. Now wiggle the toes on your other foot. Stop wiggling. Turn those toes into soft spaghetti. Good.

Wiggle one leg. Stop wiggling. Now tell that leg to go soft and sleepy like warm spaghetti. Now wiggle the other leg. Stop. Tell it to go soft and sleepy. Wiggle your bum (behind or backside). Let it go soft and sleepy.

Wiggle your fingers on one hand. Tell your fingers to stop wiggling. See if you can make those fingers feel warm and soft and sleepy like spaghetti lying on your plate. Now wiggle your fingers on your other hand. Slowly. Stop. Make those fingers feel warm. Tell them to go soft and sleepy.

Now wiggle one arm. Stop. Tell your arm to go soft and sleepy. Now wiggle the other arm. Tell it to go soft and sleepy. Good.

Let your whole you go soft and warm and sleepy like soft spaghetti lying on your plate. (Pause.) That's really good. Your body is listening well. (Pause.) Let your body stay like spaghetti and just listen to me. I want to tell you about when spaghetti toes can help you.

When you are worried or scared, or when something hurts, your toes and your hands and muscles get kinda hard and stiff—like hard spaghetti before it's cooked. If you are worried, scared or something hurts you, you feel a lot better and it doesn't hurt so much if your hands and toes and muscles are like warm, soft spaghetti lying on a plate. If you practice doing your spaghetti toes you'll get real good at it. Then you can tell your hands and toes and muscles to help you by going warm and soft and sleepy, even if you are worried or something hurts.

Before you go, let's try talking to your mouth. Wiggle your mouth. Let it go soft and sleepy. Wiggle your tongue. Let it go soft and sleepy. Wiggle your eyebrows. Let them go soft and sleepy. Let your whole you go warm and soft and sleepy. Let your whole you feel good.

Spaghetti Options—An alternate way to play this game is to ask the children to lie down and pretend they are stiff, hard pieces of uncooked spaghetti. Then go to each child and feel the stiffness in their legs and arms (if they play in pairs, partners can do this). Next, ask the children to imagine that they are sliding into a huge pot of nice warm water—like a big Jacuzzi. Tell them that by soaking in that nice warm, bubbly water their stiff spaghetti arms and legs begin to soften and relax. Ask them to feel this in their body—"Feel your body going from stiff to unstiff, from tense to relaxed." If your group is not too large you can end the game with the spaghetti test. Tell the children that you will come around and test their arms and legs by wiggling them to see if their spaghetti is done. If it is "done" their spaghetti arms and legs will be all soft and relaxed and wiggly, like cooked spaghetti. If it's not done, they may have to go back into the pot for a while.

Wiggly Arms

This activity can be done in conjunction with Spaghetti Options or it can be done independently. Usually it is played in pairs. One partner is the wiggler, the other is the wiggly. The wiggly child lies down on his back, and the wiggler takes one of his hands in her hands. She tells the wiggly child to let his arm relax and go wiggly. She holds his hand firmly and wiggles his whole arm, gently. If it is very relaxed and floppy (like cooked spaghetti), it will wiggle well. After wiggling it, she lets it drop gently onto the mat next to his side or lowers it gently onto the floor. She follows the same wiggly procedure with his other arm. She can also wiggle his hand if she places her hand firmly around his wrist and shakes his hand gently so it flops up and down. Children also like to have their legs and fingers wiggled.

Jelly Belly

This activity is designed to help children learn how to do diaphragm breathing (breathing with the abdomen or stomach). Diaphragm breathing relaxes the body and is a more efficient way of breathing than the normal chest breathing. Many classical singers and athletes are taught diaphragm breathing because of its relaxation effect and performance advantages. To introduce this activity to the children read them the following script, or use our audio-tape.

To make this activity more fun for young children, make some Jell-O together, using a mold or a bowl. Once it is set, let them wiggle it and jiggle it and then eat it before or after doing Jelly Belly.

Have you ever heard of a jelly bean? Well, this game is called Jelly Belly. It is a game you play by breathing into your own body and it's kinda like filling a bowl with jelly. It's a little tricky but I think you can do it.

Lie down and get yourself comfortable. Close your eyes, and tell your body to go loose and soft like warm spaghetti on your plate. (Pause.) Now tell the fingers on one of your hands to wiggle. Gently put that hand right on top of your belly button. Let your hand go quiet as it rests on top of your belly. Feel your hand get warm and soft.

Now let's see if you can get your hand to move up and down gently, by talking to your belly. See if you can breathe in air slowly and gently, until your belly pushes your hand up. Now see if you can breathe out slowly so that your hand sinks down on your belly. Breathe in—let your belly push your hand up slowly. Breathe out—let your hand sink down gently. As you breathe in, feel your belly slowly fill right up to your belly button. Feel your belly gently push your hand way up.

As you breathe out, let your belly sink way down until it feels empty. Feel your belly slowly pull your hand way down.

Breathe in—belly way up
Breathe out—belly way down
Breathe in—belly way up
Breathe out—belly way down
Breathe in—belly way up
Breathe out—belly way down
(Repeat the in and out phase 5 times)

Good! Now I'd like you to just breathe easily and slowly. Each time you breathe out, think to yourself, "relax." Let your whole you go soft and warm and sleepy. (Pause 30 seconds.) Good.

You feel really relaxed. You feel really good. Your body feels really good. You made your body feel good by talking to it. The more you talk to your body, the more it listens to you and the more it does what you want it to do. You are the boss of your belly and your body.

Jelly Belly on the Move—Once children have experienced Jelly Belly (diaphragm breathing), encourage them to practice it in different positions and under different circumstances. For example, after they have finished doing Jelly Belly in a lying position, give them the following instructions: Keep your hand on your belly, sit up, and see if you can still breathe easily and slowly making your jelly belly go out and in while sitting. Don't spill the jelly in the belly. Ask them to try Jelly-Belly breathing while standing, walking, talking or running.

Floating on Clouds

Lie down and get yourself into a comfortable position. Close your eyes. Breathe easily and slowly. Imagine that you are outside in a very quiet place. It is a beautiful day. Everything is warm and happy. Everything is completely quiet. You are lying down looking up at the clouds—big, white, soft, fluffy clouds—in the beautiful blue sky. As you breathe in you begin to float gently off the ground. You float up and up slowly, gently, to a big fluffy cloud in the sky. You float right up over top of the cloud and gently sink into the cloud. You are now floating on top of a big fluffy cloud. Your arms and legs are stretched out wide and you are floating on the biggest, softest cloud that is floating in the sky.

You feel so good, and so relaxed, and so calm, floating on your cloud. It makes you feel good all over. You are strong. You are happy. You are healthy. You feel as if you can do anything. You feel good energy from your cloud. Good feelings spread through your entire body and mind as you float gently, enjoying your ride on your special cloud.

FLOATING ON CLOUDS

Whenever you want to float back down to the earth, just tell your cloud and it will float you gently down, down, to the ground. Once you are safely stretched out on the ground, your cloud floats back up to its home in the sky. It smiles at you. You smile at it. Floating on your cloud is fun. Any time you want to really relax, or any time you are worried about something, you can go for a float on your cloud. Your cloud is always happy to have you visit.

Follow your Breathing

Get yourself into a comfortable position. Close your eyes and just listen to my voice. Breathe easily and slowly. Let yourself relax. Breathe in slowly. Breathe out slowly. Breathe in slowly. Breathe out slowly. For the next 3 breaths, as you breathe out say to yourself . . . Relax . . . Relax . . . Relax. Feel the relaxation spread through your body. (Pause.) Good.

Now listen closely to the sound of your own breathing. As you breathe in, listen to the sound of the air going into your body. As you breathe out, listen to the sound of the air leaving your body. (Pause for a few breaths.) Good.

Now focus on the feeling of your own breathing. As you breathe in, feel the air going into your body. As you breathe out, feel the air leaving your body. Follow the feelings of your breath going in and out. (Pause.) Good.

You are feeling good. You are feeling relaxed. You are in control. Whenever you are tense, or want to relax, follow your breathing. Breathe easily and slowly. This will free you to relax and enjoy.

Contacting Muscles

This is an activity designed to help children connect with various muscles in their body. A specific muscle is touched from the outside, and the child is asked to focus on "feeling" exactly where the muscle is, and to then get that muscle to move or respond in some way. For example, you can start with the muscle in the back part of your own lower leg—the calf muscle. Squeeze it gently but firmly a couple of times and leave your hand on the calf muscle. Try to "feel" the muscle. Then try to contract the muscle you are touching and only that muscle. Try to make it move or jump. Now wiggle the muscle back and forth with your hand. Try to let it relax. Let it go warm and soft. Let it relax.

Children can be guided through this same procedure with different muscle groups in the body. For example, the front of the upper arm, the back of the upper arm, the forearm, the shoulder muscles, the front of the thigh, the back of the thigh, the back of the neck, the hands and so on. It may take some time for children to gain control over the contraction and relaxation of all muscle groups, especially if the goal is to contract one muscle without moving other parts of the body. However, every child is capable of learning how to relax their muscles effectively, and this process will bring children one step closer to gaining control over their own minds and bodies.

Muscle Massage

Muscle massage has been used for centuries as a means of relaxation and tension release. It is an excellent way to help children learn to relax and tune in to their own bodies. This activity is best done in pairs. One partner begins by gently placing his hands on a major muscle group (such as the shoulders, neck or back) for about 30 seconds. As contact is made with that muscle group from the "outside," the receiving child is asked to "feel" that muscle, and "relax it," from the "inside." Children accomplish this by focusing on the warmth of the contact point where the hands have been placed, by thinking into the muscle and by telling that muscle to "relax." The hands remain stationary on the muscle for about 30 seconds before beginning a gentle massage. When a massage is carried out in a respectful and gentle manner, it leaves everyone feeling more physically relaxed and mentally calmer.

Muscle massage is a good opportunity for parents to spend some high quality, quiet time with their children. When children feel relaxed and secure, they are much more likely to talk openly, ask important questions and share their concerns. The chance of meaningful communication occurring is greatly enhanced when sharing quiet time together, when you are relaxed, they are relaxed, you are focused on them and you are both free from interruptions.

Magic Feet

This is a favorite massage for many children and it's also a favorite of mine. It's amazing how much feeling you have in your feet and how quickly a foot massage can relax your entire body. We pay far too little attention to our feet, especially in that they do so much for us. This activity helps make up for that omission and little people's feet will love you for it.

The receiving child lies down with legs outstretched. He'll need bare feet for this one, preferably squeaky clean or at least mud-free. Do one foot at a time. With young children start by gently wiggling each toe, and to each toe say, "hello." Next, gently slide your index finger (first finger) through the slot between each set of toes. Do this a couple of times. Spend the rest of your time massaging the bottom of the foot. Begin by massaging the underpart of each toe. Then massage the ball of the foot and slowly work your way back to the heel. There is no wrong way to massage a foot but you will get better at it faster by asking your children about their preferences. For example, ask him what part feels best and whether he would like you to massage harder or easier. With little feet you can massage the whole foot using your thumb or index finger. For those who like a firmer massage, especially on the heel, make a fist and massage that area with your knuckles. Whatever way you do it, it's magic on feet.

A hand massage is also a treat. Begin by gently massaging each finger (front, back and sides). Then focus most of your attention on massaging the entire palm of the hand. This feels best and is most relaxing. Massaging the "V" part of the hand between the thumb and index finger also has a very relaxing effect. Massage it firmly with your thumb on the top part of the "V" and your index finger underneath. For many centuries the Chinese have massaged this area as a means of inducing relaxation and removing headaches.

Relaxing with Music

Music is a great medium for relaxation and children will respond very well to it if you choose something they like. Music can elicit many types of feelings, images and emotions, some of which lead to excitement, others which lead to relaxation. Experiment with different kinds of music and observe how the children respond. Try some of the nature tapes and tranquil melodies recommended in the Resource section.

Relaxed Breathing

Get yourself into a comfortable position. Close your eyes and just listen to my voice. Breathe easily and slowly. Let yourself relax.

As you breathe in feel your chest slowly fill with air. As you breathe out, let yourself relax. Breathe in—feel your chest rise. Breath out slowly—relax. Breathe in—feel your chest rise. Breathe out—relax.

Continue to breathe easily and slowly. Feel yourself relax. As you breathe out, say to yourself "relax" . . . "relax" . . . "relax." Let your whole body relax.

Good. You are sinking deeper and deeper into a calm and wonderful state of complete relaxation.

RELAXED BREATHING

For the next few breaths continue to follow your breathing. Breathe easily and slowly. As you breathe in, allow your stomach to rise and extend. As you breathe out let your whole body relax. Breathe in—feel your stomach rise. Breathe out—relax. Breathe in—feel your stomach rise. Breathe out—relax. For the next 5 breaths each time you breathe in, feel your stomach rise—each time you breathe out, say to yourself "relax" . . . (pause 5 breaths).

Good. You are calm. You are relaxed. You feel confident and happy to be alive. You are in control. You feel great.

Whenever you want to relax, take in one long, slow, breath, and as you breathe out, think to yourself "relax." This will put you back in control.

Note: If children are expected to get up and continue with other activities after this exercise, conclude the exercise as follows:

This concludes our exercise in relaxed breathing. You've done a great job relaxing yourself. Now slowly stretch your arms to the side, open your eyes and have a great day.

Muscle Relaxation

Get yourself into a comfortable position. Close your eyes and just listen to my voice. Breathe easily and slowly. (Pause.) Let yourself relax. Feel the relaxation spread through your body. Good.

Now I'd like you to think into different body parts I mention and let those body parts relax. Let's start with your feet. Move your toes slightly. Let them relax. Now think into your lower legs. Let the muscles in your lower legs totally relax. Think into your upper legs. Let those muscles totally relax. Feel your legs sink into a completely relaxed state. Relax your behind. (Pause.)

Focus on the muscles in your lower back. Think relaxation into those muscles. Feel the relaxation spread into your upper back. Feel your whole body sink into a deep state of relaxation. Now focus on your fingers. Feel them tingle slightly. Think warmth into your fingers. Let them totally relax. Relax your lower arms, your upper arms and your shoulders. Totally relax. Relax your neck. (Pause.) And your jaw. Feel your head sink into a totally relaxed and comfortable position.

Scan your body for possible areas of tightness and relax those areas. Feel your entire body encircled with soothing warmth and relaxation. Enjoy this wonderful state of complete relaxation. (Pause one minute.)

Good. You are calm. You are relaxed. You feel confident and happy to be alive. You are in control. You feel great.

This concludes our exercise in muscle relaxation. You've done a great job relaxing yourself. Now slowly stretch your arms to the side, open your eyes and have a great day.

Special Place Relaxation

Get yourself into a comfortable position. Close your eyes and listen to my voice. Breathe easily and slowly. (Pause.) Let yourself relax. Feel the relaxation spread through your body. As you breathe out feel yourself sink deeper and deeper into a calm and wonderful state of complete relaxation. (Pause.)

SPECIAL PLACE

Now in your imagination I'd like you to go to a very special place. This is your own special place. It is the most beautiful and most relaxing place you can imagine. You can go here whenever you want to find peace and calm. In your special place it is warm, it is quiet, it is beautiful. You are totally relaxed, enjoying the warmth and calmness of your special place. (Pause.) Feel the warmth. Feel the stillness. Enjoy the silence. Enjoy the beauty.

In your special place it is so relaxing. You are calm. You are relaxed. You feel confident and happy to be alive. You are in control. You feel great.

Feel the calmness spread through your entire body and mind, as you rest gently, enjoying the peace and special feeling of your special place. You feel so good, and so relaxed. You are comfortable, you are warm, you are safe. You are in control of your body and mind. Enjoy this wonderful, restful state. Whenever you are tense remember the feeling of your special place. Go there to find peace and relaxation.

Standing Relaxation

Once children are capable of relaxing in a stretched-out position on a mat or on the floor, let them try relaxing while they are standing.

Stand up. Stretch your arms slowly over your head. Lower your arms and let them rest by your side. Face your feet forward about shoulder width apart. Bend your knees very slightly . . . just a tiny bit. Good. Now leave your hands by your sides and circle your shoulders a few times. Let your shoulders drop down and relax. Shake your arms and hands. Let them relax. Good. Now focus on your breathing. Take one long slow breath in. Breathe out slowly and think to yourself, "relax." Breathe in slowly. Breathe out letting all the tension flow out of your body.

For the next 5 breaths, continue to breathe easily and slowly. Each time you breathe out, think to yourself "relax." (Pause for 5 breaths.)

Good. You feel good. You feel great. You are relaxed. You are in control. You feel confident and happy to be alive. Stretch your arms out to the side, bring them up over your head and lower them back down to your sides. Feel all the good energy within your body. Make the best of the rest of this great day.

One-Breath Relaxation

Our goal with children is to develop their ability to relax to the point that they are able to relax quickly whenever it may be helpful. Tell them that this is the final goal for their relaxation training. Consider using the following introduction to one-breath relaxation.

Your goal is to get so good at relaxing yourself that you can relax quickly whenever you are tense, worried, upset, hurt, mad or simply want to get some good sleep. You can learn to do this by practicing one-breath relaxation. Let's start right now. When I say go, I want you to slowly breathe in, taking in one long, slow, deep breath. As you breathe in feel the air slowly filling your body. Then slowly breathe out—letting all the air and tension flow out of your body. As you breathe out, calmly say to yourself, "relax," and feel the tension leave your body. OK, let's try it. Go. (Pause—one long, slow breath in and out.)

How did you do? Let's try it one more time. Ready, go. Slowly breathe in filling your body with air. Slowly breathe out letting all the tension leave your body. Relax.

Good. Now if you want to get really good at this, every time you are facing a stressful situation or something upsets you at home, in the playground, in a game or competition, try your one-breath relaxation. Take one long, slow, deep breath in, then slowly breathe out thinking to yourself—relax.

Practice this every day, whenever something bothers you. This will put you in control of your mind, your body, your tension and your relaxation. See how good you can get at one-breath relaxation. See how many times you can use it today.

Clocking Pulse

Children really enjoy taking their pulse rates before and after relaxing. It is a good way for them to see the effect that relaxation has on their body. First, show them how to find their own pulse by gently placing the tips of their first two fingers on the underside of their wrist. If they stretch out all their fingers on one hand with their palm facing up, and look at their wrist, they will see two lines (tendons) just under the skin which are parallel to each other. Ask them to gently place two fingers just on the thumb side of those tendons. There is a little dip there and that's where they will find their pulse. They can also find their pulse in the front part of their throat, on either side of their neck. Find your own and then help them find theirs.

Before and after relaxation exercises have the children take their own pulse rates for 30 seconds or 60 seconds. Give them a signal to start and stop and let them record their findings. If you have access to a heart rate monitor—the children love using them when doing their relaxation and imagery exercises.

Cues to Relax

Parents, teachers and coaches can help children develop "cues." "triggers" or reminders that can help them relax. One way to do this is to repeat a word like "relax" to children when they are very relaxed or when they are just about to drift off to sleep. Children can also be encouraged to think of a relaxing image or repeat a word like "relax," to themselves as they exhale, while in a relaxed state. The goal here is to try to help children develop an association between breathing out or thinking "relax," and the feeling of deep relaxation. Once a meaningful association has been developed the child can use this personal cue, image or reminder to enter a more relaxed state in a variety of settings.

Coping with Stress

Our ultimate goal in teaching children relaxation and stress control skills is for them to be able to use these skills in effectively living their lives. To assist children in applying the relaxation strategies they have learned, it is helpful to let them discuss what they find stressful, what it feels like and what they can do about it. These discussions can take place one-on-one or with small groups of children. Begin by asking the children, "What kinds of things make kids feel stressed, uptight, scared, tense, nervous or worried?" "What do *you* find most stressful or worrying?" For younger children you may have to prompt them with additional questions. For example, "Are there any things you do, or things other people say or do to you, that make you feel scared, worried, sick or bad inside your stomach? Do you ever worry about making a mistake, getting yelled at, or someone finding out that you did something you weren't supposed to do? What do you worry about?" Try to get some specific examples from each child. Once you have done this, try to get a feeling for how they personally experience stress.

"How do you know when you are scared, stressed, tense, nervous or worried?"

"What does it feel like?"

"What do you feel in your mind or your body?"

"Where do you feel it?"

"How does your body react?"

Encourage the children to discuss what helps them deal with stress. Ask them, "What has worked best for you to get rid of stress or worry?" "When you have been able to let your worries go, what did you do or think about that helped you?"

Get some input from each child about how they have best prevented or handled stress. Make a list of their best strategies and suggestions. Compliment the children on the good things they are already doing to cope with stress. Thank them for sharing their good thoughts. Leave them with a few suggestions on how they might also apply other good strategies which may not have been mentioned such as Spaghetti Toes, Jelly

Belly, one-breath relaxation, positive thinking, "treeing it" or changing channels. Give very specific examples of how and where they might apply some of these positive strategies. Encourage the children to act on these strategies at the very next opportunity and follow up to find out how it worked. ❤

5

Imagine Games

Imagery is like when you think of something and all of a sudden 'pop' you're in a different world. It's really neat. (9-year-old)

It's like you're on a magic carpet. Your thoughts are nice and relaxing. You're free from everything and you let your imagination run free. (10-year-old)

You feel like you're in a dream but you're awake. You can feel things more than when your eyes are open. (10-year-old)

Imagery is like closing your eyes and going on a trip to a really special place. It's awesome. (11-year-old)

It was like I was Superwoman flying over a lake. I could hear the birds singing my favorite song. (10-year-old)

I felt like I was on the fastest horse in the world, riding it and getting lots of air, and feeling good about me. (11-year-old)

I could feel myself swimming in a big lake and the water was really fresh. It was wonderful. (9-year-old)

Can you imagine feeling something without seeing it?

Yes, it's like thunder. When it thunders you can feel it but you can't see it. It's the same as that. (8-year-old)

Why is imagination important? Imagination is important because when it is directed in positive ways it leads knowledge, creates opportunities, awakens new perspectives, provides inspiration and directs action. It is essential in pursuing positive dreams and reaching for worthy goals. It is instrumental in coping with stress and adapting to various demands. It is a wonderful medium for relaxation, regeneration, healing and creating special moments in life.

> *Imagination is more important than knowledge*
> —Albert Einstein.

Children have an amazing capacity for imaginative play and creative thinking. By recognizing this wonderful gift, and guiding them to use it in positive ways, you will ensure that it survives and flourishes. This in turn will help children become the wonderful people they can be. The imagine games in this chapter are designed to help you do this. You can introduce these activities to children by reading them the script associated with each activity, by explaining the activity in your own words, or by using our audio-tapes (see Resource section).

Leading Children into Imagine Games

When first introducing young children to imagine games, it is important to set a positive tone. I usually begin as follows:

We're going to play some fun games that are called Imagine Games. I know you will be good at these games because when you play "pretend" on your own, or play "make-believe" with a friend, you already play imagine games. Sometimes you pretend that you are a special person or make-believe that you are somebody else or something else, like an exciting cartoon character or animal. Sometimes you imagine going to special places and create wonderful things in your mind. In imagine games, when you imagine something, you pretend or make-believe that it's real. You free yourself to see, and feel, and dream about things just as if they were real.

In some of our imagine games we ask you to talk to your body, to listen to your body and to tell your body to do certain things. I know you can talk to your body because you already tell your body lots of things, like when to get up, when to sit down, how fast to run and how high to skip or jump. You can even tell your body to relax and go soft like cooked spaghetti, and your body usually listens. I also know your body can talk to you because it tells you when you are hungry, or thirsty, or tired, and when you need to have a pee. And you usually understand what your body is telling you, especially if your body talks loud enough and if you listen very closely.

Listen very closely to what you are asked to do in these imagine games and try to get your mind and body to follow.

Quiet Lake

Before beginning activities that call upon images of nature, it helps to take children into a natural setting to let them experience a quiet lake, flowing stream or floating cloud. If this is not possible then provide pictures or videos that vividly depict these images, or think of creative ways to communicate the concept.

Before doing "Quiet Lake" with a group of kindergarten children, one teacher began by giving each child a cup of water. She asked them to stir the water until it was spinning and churning around and then to stop and let the water become very still—like a quiet lake. She asked them to watch the water as it slowed down, and try to become still and quiet with the water. This helped the children understand the concept of stillness and helped them to relax. Some of the children found that they could also use a cup of water or "Quiet Lake" to relax themselves at home.

Get yourself into a comfortable position. Breathe easily and slowly. Let yourself relax. Good. Now close your eyes and just listen to my voice. Try to do what I tell you to do. Wiggle your fingers. Slowly. Stop. Now let your fingers relax. Let your arms and shoulders sink down. Wiggle your toes. Slowly. Stop. Now let your feet and legs sink down. Good. Breathe easily and slowly. Imagine that everything inside you is warm and calm and happy. Everything is completely quiet. (Pause.)

QUIET LAKE

In your mind imagine that it is a bright sunny morning. You are sitting quietly beside a beautiful lake. The sun is shining on you making you feel great all over. You can feel the rays of the sun warming you up. You are perfectly calm. The sun is shining, the air tastes good. It is a delicious morning. You can feel the warmth of the sun. You are so quiet and still that things around you reflect off you just like they reflect off a beautiful calm lake in the morning. Everything is still. Only your breath is moving. The mist is rising gently off the lake and you feel quiet, warm and very happy.

A duck swims by to say hello. It quacks twice . . . just in case you didn't hear the first quack. It makes a tiny little wave that ripples all the way across the lake. Then everything goes quiet again. Everything is calm. You feel great. When you open your eyes you will continue to feel great, no matter what you do for the rest of your day or night.

It is a good idea to do the activities together with the children. Then at the end of the exercise each person can share their experiences—what they saw, felt, heard or imagined. This promotes the sharing of feelings and helps everyone understand the variety of images that children can create. It also allows you and the children to see how their images progress over time.

The first time I did "Quiet Lake" with my daughter, I asked her if she was able to "see" a calm lake. She said, "Yeah, but then a motor boat came along and made waves." If "waves" do enter an image, encourage the children to let the waves go across the lake, and allow the lake to return to its original totally calm state.

Creating Images

Ask the children to close their eyes and to try to imagine responses to the instructions you provide.

- Imagine four different animals with tails.

- Imagine them swishing or wagging their tails back and forth.

- Imagine four things that fly.

- Imagine three animals that lay eggs.

- Imagine two sports you like.

- Imagine that you are something very colorful that flutters its wings and floats up and down in the air as it flies.

- Imagine three things that hop . . . sing . . . bark . . . howl . . . run . . . swim, etc.

Following each imagine instruction, give the children a chance to share some details of their experiences. For example, what color was the animal, what size, where was it, what was it doing, was the image clear or cloudy, etc. After the children have tried a few of your "imagine instructions," let them come up with some of their own, which they can share with the other children.

Butterfly/flutterby

Get yourself into a comfortable position. Close your eyes and just listen to my voice. Breathe easily and slowly. Let yourself relax. Good.

Imagine that you are outside on a beautiful, warm summer day. Right in front of you is a lovely butterfly, fluttering up and down. Follow the movement of its wings. (Pause.)

The butterfly lands right in front of you on a flower. Look closely at the color and shape of its wings. Notice the beautiful designs—the lines, the dark spots and light spots. As the butterfly takes off and begins to fly, imagine that its wings are moving in slow motion. (Pause.) Imagine that you are the butterfly. Feel its wings move as if they were your wings. Feel your wings move up and down in slow motion. Enjoy the feeling of gently floating through the air like a butterfly. Good.

Now open your eyes and share what you felt and saw in your butterfly imagery.

Soaring

Get yourself into a comfortable position. Close your eyes and just listen to my voice. Breathe easily and slowly. Let yourself relax. Good.

Imagine that you are outside in a beautiful place on a clear sunny day. The sky is blue. The sun is warm. You feel relaxed and happy to be alive. Just above you can see a seagull (or eagle) soaring in the sky. It's close enough to see its feathers and the tips of its wings. Look closely at the designs on its feathers.

The seagull is floating above you in the sky with its wings outstretched to the side. Every now and then, it slowly flaps its wings. They move in slow motion. You can hear the sound of its wings moving up and down. Imagine that you are the seagull. Feel its wings move as if they were your wings. Feel your wings move up and down in slow motion. Feel yourself soar gently through the air with your wings outstretched to the side. Feel the sensation of the air against your wings. Enjoy the free and wonderful feeling of gliding, floating, soaring through the sky. You feel great. You feel free. You feel relaxed. Carry this feeling with you for the rest of your day.

Note: The clarity of children's imagery in exercises such as "Butterfly" and "Soaring" can be enhanced by first showing children real butterflies or birds in flight, in the outdoors or on video. Even still pictures can help.

Finger Drawing

Ask the children to close their eyes and "draw" their name in the sand, on the ground or on the floor, using only their finger. They actually move their finger along the floor as they "draw" their name. Ask them to feel their finger making contact with the ground as it shapes each letter and to see each letter in their mind. They can also draw other things with their finger while imagining its details in their mind. This is a good introduction game for imagery because part of what the children do is real (i.e., moving their finger on the ground) and part of it lives in their imagination. Once eyes are opened, children can share the details of their "drawings." Children can also play in partners taking turns "finger drawing" letters, names, words or shapes on their partner's back. As one child "draws" with her finger, she imagines each letter or shape. As the other child feels the letter or shape being drawn on his back, he imagines each letter or shape and guesses what it is.

Clicking with Your Eyes

One way to help children learn to hold on to a visual image is to ask them to "click it" with their eyes. Ask them to imagine that their eyes are like a camera. When they see something interesting or beautiful, like a little purple flower, ask them to "click it" with their eyes. Tell them that this is to ensure that the image or picture remains inside their head (on the film in their mind). Ask the children to blink their eyes as they click the image. Clicking with the eyes is great when taking children on hikes in the woods. Whenever a child finds something of special interest, she can "click it" with her eyes and then call over a friend to share what she has clicked.

If children experience difficulty holding on to an image, they can try multiple clicks—for example, by observing a flower, clicking it, keeping their eyes closed while trying to "see" the flower in their mind, looking at it again, clicking it again until they are able to recall the image in their mind.

The concept of clicking images is not restricted to visual images. It can be used with all other senses as well. Children can be encouraged to "click" sounds, smells, tastes, sensations, feelings and emotions, using their ears, nose, touch, intuition and inner feelings. Multiple senses can be drawn into the clicking process.

Your Own Special Place

Children enjoy going to special places that are real, and they also enjoy creating their own special places in their minds or imaginations. Whether real or imagined, special places are good places to go to relax, to smile, to go on an adventure, to have fun, to unwind, to gain strength or to take a little break when feeling sad or worried.

In this game, children go on a voyage to their own very special place. They decide where their special place will be, what it looks like and how it feels to be there. Their special place can be anything they want it to be because they create it, and then visit it in their make-believe world. Their special place can be a favorite place where they have already been, or a place where they would like to go. Sometimes it is a real place, sometimes it is a pretend or make-believe place, which they make up and visit in their imagination.

One of my little friends created a special place in the land of the happy clouds where she builds fluffy little houses in the clouds, plays with colorful ponies and rides on stars. Another friend has a special place in the land of the chocolate mountain, where the mountain is made of wonderful dark chocolate, the trees dance with children, the river flows with cold milk and icicles are made of bananas, oranges and grapes.

The icicles make her strong, and she can share her strengths with others.

Another cherished friend has a special place on a huge three-layer cake, big enough to climb up on and slide around. It's her favorite kind of cake, spongy and bouncy, and covered with a very, very thick layer of whipped cream. In her mind she climbs up on her special cake, slides from layer to layer, rolls around, and jumps up and down. She likes to lick the whipped cream and have fun doing whatever she feels like doing. For her it is a very sweet adventure.

Special Place Script—*Get yourself into a comfortable position. Close your eyes and just listen to my voice. Breathe easily and slowly. Let yourself relax.*

In your imagination you are going to visit your own special place. Your own special place is a very happy place, a special place of fun and joy. It is a place where you always feel good, happy and relaxed. When you are there you are never scared or worried or upset about anything. You are never afraid to try anything. When you decide you want to do something there, you know you can do it. You always feel relaxed, good, happy and strong in your own special place. Think about your own special place. Imagine it just as you would like it to be. (Pause.) See what it looks like. Hear what it sounds like. Feel what it feels like. Taste what it tastes like. (Pause.) See it clearly. Feel it. Relax and enjoy it. (Pause 20-30 seconds.) Good. You can come back now with a smile on your face and a smile inside your body. You will remain relaxed and happy all day.

When the children return from their special place, ask them if they would like to draw or share some details about their special place. Two older children described their special place, as follows:

It is beautiful and full of love and trust and honesty. It's like nowhere but everywhere. Like the sky pure and clean. It's like the sky on a warm summer's day. There is soft fairy-like music coming from the air. Everything is calm and silent except for the music. It's like the sky. I'm in the sky and I lie on a cloud that is not there, yet supports me. It's soft and I just gently snuggle in it. Sometimes there is a rainbow or a different colored sky. It is beautiful and special. Far away you can hear the soft sound of a waterfall. Everything is peaceful and quiet.

My special place is in the forest. The sun is shining through the trees casting squinting rays all about. I'm laying in a hammock strung between two trees and I'm watching birds fly about from tree to tree lazily. Other than an occasional chirp, the brook babbling noisily is the only sound. The hammock creaks and I awake from my light sleep. It smells of freshness. That smell is indescribable and it is found only in my special place.

Star Track

This is an imaginary space voyage that unfolds differently for each child. The children really like to do this one with the audio-tape because the count-down and music set a nice tone for space travel (see Resource section). The instructions go something like this:

Get yourself into a comfortable position. Breathe easily and slowly. Let yourself relax. Close your eyes and just listen to my voice.

Today you are going on a special trip. You're going on amazing space voyage—to the stars. You are the captain of this spaceship and you are ready to begin the voyage (countdown—10, 9, 8, 7, 6, 5, 4, 3, 2, 1 – Ignition – Blastoff!) You are off on your trip to the stars. Feel yourself going up and up, further and further into space, closer and closer to the stars. Feel yourself moving quickly through space. See the colors zooming by around you. (Pause.) Pick a star that you'd like to go to. Watch that star. Notice the color of that star. As you get closer, and closer, everything slows down. You are floating gently over the surface of that star. You are free. You are weightless, moving in slow motion. Have a look around. Feel the warm light from your star gently touch you. Float in its light. Feel the good energy. (Pause.) Now take 2 long, slow deep breaths and beam yourself back to earth.

Once everybody is safely back on earth, ask the children if they would like to share something about their experience. Go around the circle and give every child the opportunity to answer a couple of the following questions:

- Can you us something about your trip?

- Where did you go?

- What happened out there?

- How did you feel?

- What did you see?

- What colors did you see?

- What temperature was it? (like summer, winter, spring)

- What time of day was it? (morning, afternoon, night)

- What did you do?

- Did anything special happen out there?

- Was it fun?

Magic Wands and Rainbows

This script was originally developed for children with life-threatening illnesses to give them some sense of control over their lives and their capacity to heal themselves.

Get yourself into a comfortable position. Let yourself relax. Close your eyes and quietly listen to my voice, just like a teddy bear would.

We are going to play an imagine game that can help you get stronger when you are not feeling so strong, and make you feel better when you are not feeling so good. This is an imagine game that can work for real.

Before we begin the game let me tell you a little story. You have magical powers in your body that make you grow strong and healthy. Your amazing powers can fix cuts and bruises, and make colds or hurts go away. You have millions of good things inside you to fight away the bad things. You have millions of good things that can give you strength. You can help your body get stronger and heal itself better by talking to it, by encouraging it and by imagining your body doing good things for you. You can remind your body that it is strong and powerful by saying, "I am strong and powerful." You can help your body get better and stronger, by imagining and feeling all the good things inside you working together to give you strength. You can help your body "turn on" its amazing powers by playing imagine games like "magic wands" or "rainbows." Let's start by playing rainbows.

Rainbows—*Imagine that you are outside in a beautiful place, resting quietly. You feel good. You feel safe. Everything is quiet. You feel special and know that your family loves you very much. You look up at the sky and see a beautiful, big rainbow full of different colors. Can you see it? It's red and yellow and orange and some other nice colors too. This is a very special rainbow. It has special powers and it's coming to visit you. One end of the rainbow comes right down from the sky and touches you. It shines a warm and wonderful color right through you. You can feel its special energy going through your whole body. It makes your insides tingle. It makes you feel good. You feel strong and bright. You feel healthy. You feel good about yourself. You feel good about your body. You feel great. You feel the rainbow turn on your own amazing powers inside your own body. You feel your body getting stronger and stronger. You feel all the good things inside your body taking over and making you feel strong and healthy and happy.*

Note: Some children also enjoy climbing up on the rainbow, and having a good look around from way up high, before sliding back down. Sometimes they gain a better perspective on things with distance or by moving a step away.

Magic Wand—*Now let's play a game called "magic wand." Imagine that you are floating on a big, fluffy, white cloud. You are so relaxed and comfortable stretched out on your fluffy white cloud. Lying right next to you on your cloud is a magic wand with a bright star on the end of it. Reach over and pick it up. This magic*

MAGIC
WANDS

wand is for you. You can use it to turn on the amazing powers inside your body. Take the magic wand in your hand, raise it above your head and shake it. With each shake, magical stardust floats down and fills every part of your body, bringing to life all the strength and good energy you have inside you. Feel all the good things working inside your body. Feel yourself getting better and better, stronger and stronger, more and more confident. Feel good about yourself. Feel good about your body. Feel good about the strength and power you have within you. Good!

You are getting very good at these imagine games. Remember, when you imagine your body getting stronger and better, your body actually gets stronger and better. Your body listens to your thoughts, your voice and your imagination. When you think and imagine good things, you help yourself do good things and feel good things. When you think happy thoughts and imagine the good things inside you, you feel stronger and better and happier.

You have done well today. Now it's time to take a break. Before you get up, imagine doing something that is lots of fun to do. See if you can do it today.

Space Robots

This is an activity for young children that is often initially played in a wide open space outdoors or in a large gym.

Children are asked to imagine that they are special space robots of the future. When their key is turned on, their powerful engine starts, their body runs beautifully and goes as fast as they want. When their key is turned off, their engine stops and they immediately fall to rest. "I wonder if you can do that?" After presenting children with the challenge of becoming a space robot, introduce the imaginary key. To start the engine, gently touch the side (or back) of the child with your finger and turn "the key." "There, now your engine is on." To stop the engine, turn the key in the opposite direction. "There, now your engine is resting."

On many occasions I have turned keys off and witnessed children sink into a heap on the floor and totally relax in seconds. I've also used this key successfully to help children sleep, but be sure you turn the key in the right direction. When turned the wrong way it cranks up extra energy for doing very active things.

The secret of this activity lies in helping children create an image that allows them to change mental channels. They energize by turning their image in one direction, and relax by turning it in another direction.

Once children are familiar with this activity, give each of them their own imaginary key. Tell them they can turn their engine on, up or off, whenever they want with their own imaginary key.

Step into My Red Dancing Shoes

Lots of imaginary play occurs naturally by providing children with various kinds of "props" such as big people's "dress-up" clothes, costumes, scarves, masks, helmets, hats, flippers, horns, tails, noses, wigs, boots or old shoes. Children can also create *imaginary* "props" when playing games like "Step into My Red Dancing Shoes." In this game you place a pair of imaginary red dancing shoes in front of each child and encourage them to step in, one foot at a time.

Set the scene by warning the children that these dancing

shoes start really moving as soon as you step into them. These shoes lead you all over the place . . . any place and any way they feel like going. They twirl you and spin you and jump you into the air. The only way to stop is to step out of the shoes. As the children prepare to step into their shoes, put on some energetic red-dancing-shoe music. Remind them to let the shoes lead and see where it takes them. A similar game can be played with big floppy clown shoes—imaginary ones, of course.

Another option is to ask children to step into shoes that carry different emotions. For example, sad shoes, happy shoes, confident shoes, cautious shoes or Tarzan's shoes. First describe the person who lives in these shoes. Then ask the children to step into this person's shoes in order to step into this person's feelings.

Imagine Light—Imagine Heavy

Children begin this game by placing both arms straight out in front of them, with both palms up. Ask them to close their eyes and imagine that you are placing a very heavy book (like a huge dictionary) in their left hand. Ask them to imagine that you are tying a red helium balloon to the thumb on their right hand. The balloon is floating gently up into the air. Repeat the instructions several times: "Imagine the heavy dictionary pressing down your left hand and the floating balloon pulling up your right hand." After 30 seconds ask them to "freeze" their arms where they are and to open their eyes. Let them discuss what they felt in their images, what happened to their arms and why they think that happened.

Ski Course Imagery

In many activities in sport and life it is important to have a clear image of the course or path you want to follow. This is particularly important in sports like downhill skiing and cross country equestrian events. You must know where you want to go in order to get there. Kerrin Lee Gartner, the 1992 Olympic champion in downhill skiing, ran the Olympic course hundreds of times in her mind before she actually raced that course. When I began working with Kerrin eight years earlier, as her mental training coach, her imagery skills were at a basic level. By the time she arrived at the Olympics her imagery skills were amazing.

To prepare for a race, Kerrin carefully inspects the course terrain, the bumps, the turns, the flats, the drops, the overall lay of the land, and decides upon the best path to follow. She slides down the hill a few gates at a time looking very closely at the terrain, choosing her path and then closing her eyes to imagine her path in her mind. By the time she gets to the bottom of the course inspection she has already seen and run every section of the course in her mind and some sections have been experienced 25 or 30 times in her imagery. Her coach also draws a map of the course which she uses as a reference point for imagery.

To introduce children to the concept of using imagery to learn courses, or paths to follow through life, the following activities are suggested.

On a piece of normal sized paper (i.e., typing, notebook or computer paper), draw a simple "S" shaped pattern from the top of the page to the bottom. Limit this course to three or four wide easy "S" turns which follow the same pattern all the way down. Draw a second "S" shaped line parallel to the first all the way down the page. Leave about one inch between the lines. The "S" shaped path between these two lines is the course that the children will attempt to imagine and follow in this exercise. Make sure the course is simple and rhythmical in nature. Another simple course option to begin with is a zigzag course.

Once the children have their course map in hand, inform them that their challenge is to trace or follow that course with their eyes closed. Then let them experiment with different imagery options to learn the course.

1. **Visual Imagery**—Look at the course very carefully. Keep your eyes open and follow the course with your eyes from one end to the other (top to bottom). Do this four or five times. Then close your eyes and try to imagine the course in your mind. Keeping your eyes closed, try to follow the course from one end to the other as you did with your eyes open. Then open your eyes, pick up your pencil and place it at the start of the course. Close your eyes and see how closely you can follow the path of the course with your pencil.

2. **Feeling Imagery**— Look at the course carefully. Keep your eyes open and follow the course with your fingers from one end to the other. Actually place the tips of your first two fingers on the paper and run them through the course. Do this four or five times. Then close your eyes and try to run your fingers through the course. Do this four or five times,

opening your eyes only to replace your fingers at the start of the course. Then open your eyes, pick up your pencil and place it at the start of the course. Close your eyes and see how closely you can follow the path of the course with your pencil.

3. Moving Imagery—This activity is designed to allow children to move through simple courses that they have imagined in their minds. Place four marker cones in a straight line, leaving about four or five steps between each marker. Ask the children to stand at the first marker and to imagine themselves walking through the markers on the outside of each cone (weaving through the gates). They can first imagine their path with their eyes open, then with eyes closed. Suggest that they look exactly where they want to go. "Let your eyes follow the exact path you intend to follow, and imagine the number of steps you will take between markers." Once they have completed their course in imagery, ask them to close their eyes and walk through the course keeping their eyes closed (either alone or holding onto a sighted partner).

See if the children can imagine themselves moving through different types of real courses. First ask them to imagine the course or path they want to follow, then ask them to try to imagine themselves walking, skiing, running, sliding, biking or swimming through the course, from one end to the other.

As children's imagery skills improve, the courses they "run" mentally can become more elaborate and complex. They can draw upon progressively more challenging courses to run in their minds and with their bodies, and they can create their own paths to follow in different domains of their life.

Imagine Everyday Things

Children can be asked to "imagine" all sorts of everyday things. Imagine how you are going to get up from where you are sitting to get a drink. Imagine how you are going to walk across the room to the next room. Imagine the path you will follow to go to school, to a friend's house or to get home. Imagine how you will open the door, say hello, go down the stairs, run along the road, or hug your Mom. Imagine doing one thing you want to do today at recess, after school or after chores. Run that one thing through your mind, then do it today.

Imagine your path in as much detail as possible. This will enhance imagery skills and performance skills, and will allow children to actually do some of the things they really want to do well.

Target Images

Children are asked to look at a target, to close their eyes and "hold" an image of that target in their mind, and then to propel an object at the target, keeping their eyes closed. "Target Images" can be used when throwing balls at a target area on the wall, when serving balls, when shooting balls at hoops or propelling pucks at a specified target area. Imagining a target gives children practice at creating and holding a clear image of the target in their minds and can have a positive effect on performance. Children become more accurate when throwing or serving balls at targets when a clear image of the target remains in their minds. Performing with eyes closed is one way to help children create a clear image of what to focus on, and is also a good way of removing outside distractions.

Acting on Good Decisions

Sometimes children have to make decisions about whether or not to do something, go somewhere, follow another's lead, assert themselves, join a group, go along with peer pressure, express their view, participate in an activity or continue with a program. Encourage youngsters to take some time to think about what *they* really want to do, what is best for them and to make their final decision in the absence of outside pressure.

Once a child has made a decision that represents her best interest, she often has to communicate that decision to others, who may or may not support her decision. It is helpful to give youngsters a little practice at responding in the way they would prefer to respond, before they face a potentially stressful or uncomfortable situation. One way to do this is to ask them to imagine themselves in the real situation, responding the way they would prefer to respond. Another possibility is to set up an imaginary role-play situation where the child sits in one chair facing another chair. The other chair is actually empty but it is filled in imagination. The child says what she has to say, clearly and firmly, looking directly at the "person" in the empty chair. After finishing she switches chairs and responds, by acting and answering as she imagines this other person might respond. She then switches back to her original chair and answers in the manner she would prefer to respond.

A third possibility is to set up a real role-play situation where the child imagines herself in the real situation and either you or someone else plays the role of the child or adult with whom she must communicate her decision. In all cases the goal is for the child to gain practice at communicating her decision in a confident, polite and firm manner, and to then act upon her own decision. It is a simple way of helping children to mentally prepare themselves to respond to others in the way they would prefer to respond.

By giving children practice at responding in ways that are respectful of their own views with little things now, they will gain experience in learning how to respond in line with their own values and beliefs. This will enable them to communicate important decisions and respond in ways that are in their own best interest with bigger things later, for example, when faced with peer pressure to smoke, drink, use drugs, partake in unwanted sex or engage in inconsiderate or illegal acts. The goal here is to teach them that they decide what they choose to do or not do, and that they are capable of directing and following through with their own decisions.

Flowing Stream

This script is really about perspective—keeping things in perspective and keeping a sense of balance in your life. It is relevant at all ages. The audio-tape is accompanied by the natural sounds of a flowing stream (see Resource section).

Get yourself into a comfortable position. Close your eyes and just listen to my voice. Breathe easily and slowly. Let yourself relax. Good.

Imagine that you are outside relaxing next to a beautiful little river or stream. Listen to the relaxing sounds of the water flowing gently down the stream. Let those relaxed feelings flow through your own body. (Pause.) Now listen to your own breathing. Breathe in slowly. Breathe out slowly. Follow the sounds of your easy, relaxed breathing (for five breaths).

Now focus on listening to the relaxing sounds of the water flowing gently down the stream. Let those relaxed feelings flow gently through your own body. (Pause.) Continue to relax while I tell you a little story. If you watch water flowing down a river or stream, you will see that it always finds a path. It finds its own path, even if there are big rocks, or branches, or logs along the way. Without much worry it flows around rocks and other obstacles. It keeps flowing towards its destination. You can flow around obstacles, barriers, worries or setbacks in your day and in your life, just like a river. There are ways around, or through, almost all obstacles if you relax and let yourself flow. So, if ever you are discouraged with yourself or upset about something, imagine that you are like a little stream or powerful river. You are like the water flowing gently down that river. Allow yourself to relax and flow. Let your relaxation and calmness flow you around the obstacles and through the worries, towards your destination.

Continue to believe in yourself along the way.
Continue to believe in what you are doing.
Continue to believe in your own value.
Continue to flow along even if there are obstacles.
Follow your own path.　　　　❤

6

Focusing Activities

FOCUSING is . . .

paying attention to what you are doing right now and leaving distractions in the background. (9-year-old)

thinking of something you're supposed to think of and not something you're not supposed to think of. (7-year-old)

when you concentrate on what you're doing and don't pay attention to anything else. (8-year-old)

When you're reading, it's like stepping into the book and being there. (11-year-old)

When you're at baseball and you're at bat you have to think about what you're doing and nothing else. (7-year-old)

If you're in a race and you're losing, you don't think about it, you just keep running. (8-year-old)

When is it difficult to FOCUS?

When my teenage brother always comes into the room to look at himself in the mirror.

When my cousin throws shoes at me when I'm doing my homework.

When a car goes by in street hockey.

Focusing (or total concentration) is the most important mental skill affecting learning and performance. By developing the skills necessary to focus fully and constructively, you directly influence the quality of children's learning, performance and living. Children will learn to focus effectively through guidance and practice at connecting fully with essential things that are going on in the present moment.

There are many things we look at that we never really see. There are many sounds we hear that we never really listen to. There are many experiences we live through that we never fully live. Living fully centers around being "all here" when we are here, looking closely at what we see, listening intently, really feeling what we are feeling, connecting completely in our interactions with others, focusing fully on what we are doing and thoroughly freeing ourselves to experience what we are engaged in.

You can help children learn to focus in ways that allow them to connect totally with someone or something through the following focusing activities. The activities are designed to encourage children to absorb themselves in what they are doing, learning and experiencing. By introducing these activities to children you will nurture their ability to focus in the present, on the immediate task, to the exclusion of irrelevant internal thoughts or external distractions. This is important in all human endeavors. The ultimate goal is for children to learn to focus so well that they can remain positively focused for the duration of the lesson, experience, outing, task, exercise, game, event, performance or interaction, in a variety of situations. If children learn to do this effectively, they will gain a distinct advantage in playful ventures, academic pursuits, interpersonal relations, creative activities, physical challenges and joyful living.

Focus on Seeing

Without looking, can you describe or draw the face of your watch in detail? You've probably looked at that watch face a thousand times, without ever really seeing all of it. This may not be very important with a watch face, but if you have looked at a person a thousand times without ever really seeing or knowing her, or hear a voice a thousand times without ever really listening in detail to what that person is saying, *that is important.*

Leaf Connection

For many years, every autumn when the leaves are in full bloom, I have gone out and gathered colorful leaves. I distribute one leaf to each of the students in my class and ask them to study their leaf very carefully. I want them to absorb themselves in its designs, colors and textures. I want them to connect totally with that leaf. I tell them in advance that after they have examined their leaf very closely, we will mix all their leaves together and they will then try to find their own leaf. Knowing they will have to find their own leaf helps to intensify their focus. The amazing thing is that when they make an effort to really focus on their individual leaves, they all end up finding their own leaf, even with groups as big as fifty or sixty people.

You can use leaves from different trees, which makes it very easy, or take all the leaves from the same tree, which increases the need to focus well. You can even take fallen leaves from a single bush, where at first glance they all look exactly the same. If children look closely they will discover that each leaf is different and distinct, and they will be able to find their own leaf among many other leaves from the same bush

I have played this focusing game with all kinds of different things, for example, apples, peaches, pears and grapes. I once distributed a basket of 45 apples to a group of students, and asked each student to focus on his or her own apple. I then collected all the apples, mixed them all together and asked them to find their own apple. They did it! We concluded the game by all eating our apples, focusing on the sound of the crunch, and thoroughly enjoying the juicy sweet taste.

Within families, it's easy to play this focusing game and you don't need 45 apples. You can distribute one apple (or one grape) to each family member (and any visiting friends) and ask each person to focus on his or her own apple. Then mix them up and see if they can find their own piece of fruit.

This game works with almost anything—carrots, new tennis balls, golf balls, small rocks or even raisins—if the children focus very intently and the group is not too large.

Focus on Flakes

Just for fun, take out 10 corn flakes. Any 10 will do (as long as they are not soggy). Pick out any one of those corn flakes as your own corn flake. Look at it *very closely* for at least 15 or 20 seconds. Then mix it around with the remaining nine corn flakes and see if you can find your corn flake. Try the same game with your children and see how they do. If they are successful, they get to eat all 10 of those uniquely individual crunchy little flakes. You can also use Rice Krispies, honey nut flakes, Wheaties, Cheerios or potato chips.

When first playing this game with very young children, you might want to examine the flake together to check out its details. Look at it from the front, back and side. Discuss, or point out, its overall shape, its holes, valleys, mountains or any distinguishing features. Once the children have looked at their own flake "very closely," encourage them to close their eyes and imagine, or picture, their flake in their mind. Then ask them to open their eyes to have another look before you mix the flakes together for the focus hunt.

There are all sorts of opportunities to practice and apply focusing skills in the outdoors. Have a close look at the inside of a flower, a blade of grass, a spider, bug, frog or a small piece of bark on a tree. If you are lucky enough to live in a climate where it snows in the wintertime, snowflakes provide a special occasion for focusing. When big soft snowflakes are falling, it is possible to focus on them for brief periods as they slowly descend to earth. A close look shows you that each snowflake is beautiful and different. We often end this game by trying to get a falling snowflake to land on our tongue, which is both cool and fun.

Cloud Things

A great way to slow things down and live in the present moment is to take time to look at the clouds. One of our favorite outdoor focusing activities is watching clouds float across the sky. It can be very relaxing. When playing this game we often stretch out on the grass or a picnic table and look for special clouds in the sky. Children find all sorts of images in clouds, including crocodiles, bears, dancing people, paintings and hats on heads. Once children identify a cloud that they find interesting, ask them to watch how it changes shape as it moves across the sky. If they watch closely they will see their crocodile cloud close its wide open mouth or see their bear cloud merge with another cloud and double its size. They will see some clouds disappear completely and other clouds float past one another in opposite directions (for example, when high clouds float in one direction and low clouds float in exactly the opposite direction). Children enjoy talking about the cloud things they see and it's a good exercise in focusing. Following birds that are soaring in the sky also provides an uplifting opportunity for focusing.

A nighttime focusing alternative is to focus on shadows. It is especially fun to play together in the outdoors on moonlit nights. The children remain very still and look for interesting shadows to focus on and then share their shadowy discoveries.

High Intensity Focusing

Take out a magnifying glass on a sunny day and demonstrate to the children how the sun's rays can be narrowed to a single concentrated focus so strong that it burns a hole through a piece of paper. This is the strength of focused energy. The energy within each of us can become extremely powerful when focused in a single direction or zeroed in on a specific goal. Pick an object or goal for the children to focus on. Tell them: "Focus on it intensely, like a single ray of the sun."

Face-to-Face

This game is played in partners. Start by sitting across from your partner, face to face. Focus on each other's face, closely studying its shapes and contours. Look into each other's eyes, focusing on the colors and the way the colors blend into each other. Then describe to each other what you have seen, in detail. The goal is to develop the ability to look at something very closely, like an artist might look at it, focusing on every minute detail, painting a picture of it in your mind. Young children also enjoy playing face-to-face with their teddy bears.

There are other "people things" to focus on as well. Children can examine their partner's hand or ear, then close their eyes and try to recall the details in their mind. They can be asked to describe some of the major features they have discovered. They might recall the prints on the palm of the hand, the path of a vein, the texture of tiny hairs or the sequence of freckles on the back of their partner's hand, or the exact shape of his ear lobe.

Wood provides another opportunity for focusing. By looking closely at the grain in wood, children discover a variety of designs, patterns, knots and color changes. A small section of a clear wooden table, chair, floor, ceiling or just a plain old board, plank or hunk of firewood all work well.

Focus with Your Ears

Inside Listening

Shh . . . Listen! Make the room quiet by turning off the television, radio and major appliances. Then sit with the children and listen. Focus on the different sounds you hear—for example, the ticking of a clock, the sound of the fridge, a drip from the tap. Share the different sounds that each of you hears, focusing on that one sound, then shifting to another.

Outside Listening

Go outside to a park or beach or into your backyard or the schoolyard. Sit quietly with the children and play "the listen game." Listen closely for the different sounds you hear . . . a bird, a frog, a different bird, a cricket, a trickling stream, crashing waves, a creaking tree, the wind, people chattering or leaves fluttering. Ask the children to focus on one sound and listen closely before going on to another sound. Share your discoveries.

Body Sounds

Ask the children to sit or lie quietly, close their eyes and listen for different sounds they can hear within their own body. For example, ask them to focus on listening to their own breathing, their heartbeat, gurgles in their stomachs or the sound of swallowing. They can also listen to partner sounds. For example, one child can place his ear on the back, chest or stomach of his partner and listen closely for the sound of his heartbeat, his breathing, gurgles in his stomach or the sound of swallowing water. Children take turns listening to their partner's sounds.

Listen with Your Antennas

To begin this activity with young children ask them to sit down or lie down quietly, to close their eyes and relax their bodies. Then give them the following instructions:

Imagine that your ears are antennas that can stretch out far beyond this room.

Stretch your antennas out to wherever you would like them to go and listen to sounds you hear there. (Pause 30 seconds.) Good.

Now shorten your antennas. Bring them back into this room and listen to the sounds you can find in here. (Pause 20 seconds.) Good.

Now turn your antennas inward so you can listen to the sounds inside yourself. Listen to what you hear in your own body. Listen to your inside sounds. Listen to your own thoughts. (Pause 20 seconds.) Good.

Now stretch your arms out and lift your eyebrows up. Get into a circle and share the sounds you heard. What did you hear with your antennas outside? What do you hear with your antennas inside the room? What did you hear with your antennas inside your own body?

After each question give everyone a chance to share something they heard. Ask the listeners to point their antennas towards the person talking so they can really listen to what she says.

Before playing this game with young children you may want to explain that an outside antenna is a very sensitive organ or instrument, similar to a television antenna or satellite dish that can pick up signals or sounds from far away—even from space. An inside antenna is similar to a microphone or stethoscope used by doctors to hear sounds inside the body.

Sound Guessing

This is a game of guessing sounds. Ask the children to close their eyes, to listen to a sound and try to guess what it is. For example, you might shake some keys, snap your fingers, "ping" a pot, break a piece of spaghetti or roll a marble. Let the children take turns inventing sounds to guess and guessing sounds.

Pouring with Your Ears

In this game children attempt to fill a cup with water to the top, but not over the top, with their eyes closed. They can pour the water from a pitcher or put the cup under a tap. They accomplish their task by listening very closely to the sound of the water entering the cup. In the beginning it is best to try this game outside, in a bathtub, over a sink or container that will catch the possible overflow. To simplify the task, you (or a partner whose eyes are open) can do the pouring while the child does the listening. With an ear next to the cup and eyes closed, the child tells you when to stop pouring, and you listen closely.

Sound Listening

It's fun for children to focus on unique sounds such as the sound of loons, wolves, whales, lions or cats purring. Sometimes it is possible to focus on unique sounds like this in the real world. However, you can also bring these sounds to children on recordings. On our Feeling Great audio-tapes we include a collection of many interesting sounds that children enjoy listening to (see Resource section). When children are presented with these sounds, remind them to focus on listening closely. Then ask them to share their feelings about how the sounds feel to them and what the sounds might mean. Cats purring provide an example. When I listen to, and feel, cats purring, I often think that people should learn to purr. It seems like such a clear and simple way to communicate feelings of security, happiness and total contentment.

Connecting Through Music

The focus here is on listening to, and feeling, music. Select a piece of music or a song that you think the children will like and ask them to try to connect with the music in the following ways.

- Feel the rhythm or beat of the music in your body.

- Listen to the words of the song.

- Feel the meaning of the words.

- Feel the emotion or feelings of the singer or musicians.

After listening to the song ask the children to share what they heard and felt, as well as what they felt the singer or musician was trying to communicate. Help them to focus on what is being said by the words and to focus on understanding feelings that are often left unsaid.

Great Little Listener

The following script can be read or played on audio-tape to children during a quiet time to introduce them to the importance of good listening.

You can be a great listener if you try. Lots of big people never learned to listen very well. That's because when they were little no one really helped them learn how to do it. That can be kind of sad, especially when you have something exciting to share or when you're feeling sad about something, and you know that your mom or dad or teacher or friend isn't really listening. If you are lucky enough to have someone who really listens to you then you know how good that can make you feel.

There are lots of good reasons to learn to be a great listener. One reason is that it's fun to listen to things like dinging bells, crunching leaves, howling winds, chirping birds, roaring animals, cool songs and interesting people. Another good reason for listening is because it is the best way to know how people are really feeling and to learn from what they know. The more you listen, the more you learn.

If you decide to be a really good listener you will make your family, friends and teachers feel good, just by listening to them, and that will make you feel good too. To become a really good listener, each day say to yourself, "I'm going to really listen closely today." Then really try to do it. As you get better and better at listening you can start to help others learn to listen better too, by listening to them and by telling them how you do it. You might share some of your ideas on how to really listen with your dad, your mom, some of your friends, your teacher and even a good dog. On second thought, maybe you don't have to tell the dog because good dogs are already good listeners. Maybe you should ask the dog how she learned to listen so well.

When one teacher played this audio-tape to a group of children who had concentration problems, she realized that although everyone tells these children to "Pay Attention," no one really teaches them how to do it. Following the tape, together with the children, she discussed how to pay attention, for example by taking everything off their desk, relaxing and really trying to listen (or focus) on what someone is saying. Although these children were classified as having attentional deficit disorders they listened remarkably well to our audio-tapes and benefited greatly from them.

People Sounds

To gain fully from what another person has to share, or really understand that person, it is important to listen attentively. "People Sounds" is an exercise in listening. Two people pair up and take turns listening closely as his/her "partner" talks. The talking can be about anything that partner chooses—a highlight, a yummy dessert, a good friend, a feeling, a worry, a dream, a movie, a program or a favorite place. After listening attentively, the listening partner tries to relay back to the talking partner exactly what she has heard and felt.

A Listening Lesson

This is a good listening exercise for children to play with parents or teachers. It's also a good one for helping children learn to listen more attentively to each other. The game is played in pairs. One partner is the listener and the other is the talker. Partners sit facing one another looking directly at each other. The role of the talker is to share something that is important to her. It can be something she has done, something she wants to do, a feeling about something, a concern or a memorable experience.

For about a minute the listener does his very best to listen very attentively. Then he clearly shifts focus and becomes a poor listener. He looks at his watch, looks at the floor, picks up a book or looks at the newspaper. The talker tries to continue to talk for another minute. This is difficult to do when someone isn't listening, as they will soon discover. Partners then shift roles and repeat the exercise.

At the conclusion of the exercise, children and adults share their feelings on some of the following questions:

- How did you feel when you were being listened to for the first part of the exercise?

- How do you know when someone is really listening to you? (What do they do to make you feel listened to?)

- How did you feel when your partner started doing other things and stopped listening?

- How do you know when someone is not really listening to you? (What do they do to make you feel not listened to?)

- How can you make sure you are a really good listener?

Copy Chat

This game increases the necessity to focus on listening closely. We play it in groups of two, three, four or more. The higher the number of people the more difficult the challenge. Player one begins by talking out loud about anything he chooses, for example, a story, an experience, or something he would like to do. Player two repeats exactly what the first person says, word for word. Player three then repeats exactly what person two says, and player four repeats what person three says. As soon as the second player finishes repeating the first sentence from player one, player one continues on with the next sentence in his story. Thus there is constant talking and constant distractions. The goal of the first person is to focus only on telling his story, clearly and slowly, without being distracted by the other voices. The goal of the remaining players is to focus only on listening to, and then repeating, what the previous person says without being distracted by the other voices. This game can also be played by repeating different sounds, verses, songs or languages.

Barnyard

In this game children are divided into small groups, each of which is comprised of four or five children. Each group decides upon an animal sound that will allow them to regroup. The children then spread out all around the room or play area and try to regroup solely through the sound of their animal, with all eyes closed. This is an exercise in focusing on a unique sound in the midst of many other unique sounds, and it's lots of fun to play.

Animal Round-Up

Begin by dividing the children into groups of four. Three children in each group decide upon what kind of animal he/she would like to be—for example, one child might be a rhino, another a giraffe and the third, a horse. The fourth child in each group is designated as the animal caller and her job is to regroup her three animals by voice. The animals must keep their eyes closed and be guided by verbal instructions (for example, "giraffe move two steps forward, rhino three steps to the side, horse four steps backwards"). The instructions continue until all groups are reunited. The challenge and the fun of this game is to hear and respond to your caller's instructions in the midst of instructions from the other callers, along with the bumping and grunting of other animals.

Fun Focus

Let the children select something to do that may look funny or odd to others such as rolling a ball through a course with their nose, talking to an imaginary teammate, or walking an imaginary dog. With others watching, challenge the children to "just focus on doing what you are doing and nothing else."

Balloon Focus

Fill a small balloon with water. Partners face one another, standing about one arm's length apart, and toss the water balloon back and forth. When throwing, ask them to focus on gently tossing the balloon into their partner's hands, guiding it with their eyes, images and focus. When receiving, ask them to concentrate on following the balloon with their focus and to gently receive the balloon by "giving" (going with the momentum) as they catch it. After two tosses at one distance each partner takes a small step back. This is a good one to play outside on a warm day.

Taste Test

This is a fun game to play while sitting around the kitchen table. All you need are some goodies to taste and some willing tasters. In turn, each player closes his eyes, opens his mouth wide and sticks out his tongue. His tongue serves as a conveyor belt for little goodies that are drawn into the mouth for the taste test. Based on the feel and taste of the goodie in his mouth, he tries to guess what it is. It might be a small piece of any kind of fruit or vegetable, a grape, a piece of apple, a small carrot, a kernel of corn or a pea. It could be a pinch of sugar, salt or cinnamon; a drop of vinegar, ketchup or mustard; a sip of juice; a grain of rice; a flake of cereal; a Smartie, M & M or chocolate chip; or a spoonful of ice cream. Anything you have around the house or classroom that is safe and good to eat is fine. Try to pick a couple of things that can be identified easily, another that provides a good challenge and one that is funny or unusual, like a peeled grape.

Children can also close their eyes and use their nose to identify various items, such as mint leaves, fresh bread, apple pie, sliced banana, peanut butter, toothpaste, perfume, pine cones, pine needles and so on. Make sure you smell it yourself first to ensure that it gives off some odor or scent. One time we played the "nose knows" at a family gathering and the children suggested trying to identify different people in the family by smell. I thought it might be a little risky but it worked well and there were lots of laughs. Later on that day one of the children came up to me and said, "You know what I discovered. Nobody thinks that they smell. They think everybody else smells. But everybody has their own smell."

Mystery Object Touch

This is similar to the tasting game except the receiving child closes her eyes and a secret object is placed in her hand (or hands). She tries to guess what it is. It might be a pencil, a coin, a toothbrush, a piece of fruit, a vegetable, a corn flake, a grain of rice, an egg, an acorn, a leaf, a marble, a watermelon or any other safe object you can find inside or outside, that will fit into her outstretched hands. If you look around the house, school or any outdoor setting, you will find some really good choices for the mystery object. Make sure you also take your turn closing your eyes and trying to guess the object your child has placed in your hand. The "mystery object touch" can also be played by placing several items in a bowl on the table. The children are instructed to try to find a specific item in the bowl through touch, keeping their eyes closed.

Focus with Your Hands

This activity involves focusing with your hands. It can be played in groups of three, four or five people. The larger the number in the group, the more difficult the challenge. To begin the game one child is designated as the finder and another child is designated as "the hand." The finder closes her eyes and "the hand" places one of his hands in the finder's hands. She examines his hand closely, trying to discover its uniqueness, texture, feel, size, length, shape and temperature. Once she has a good feel for that hand, she indicates that she is ready for the search. One by one other members of the group extend one hand to the finder which she examines with her eyes closed until she feels she has found the original hand.

When playing this game with family members or with groups of people who know each other very well, the finder can try to identify each person in the group by the feel of their hand. In this case the finder can look at and touch each person's hand before she begins the search. To increase the challenge and add some fun, see if they can identify a person by the feel of their ear, wrist, thumb or face. The ear works well as long as someone guides the finder's hand to each ear. The size, shape, texture or even a tiny bump on the back of an ear lobe can lead you to your find. With a group of more than four or five you might want to get a couple of finders going at the same time. When someone guesses correctly, it is interesting to hear about (or feel for yourself) what they focused on to make their find.

Bodytalk

We begin life with little or no control over certain body functions. For example, when the bladder begins to fill, the urine simply exits, anywhere, anyplace, any time. Over time we learn to focus within our bodies, to recognize certain impending signals and go to the bathroom in a specified place, at an appropriate time. We accomplish this by learning to "listen," and "talk," to our bodies. Even with very complex internal functions our bodies can learn to listen.

Children have the capacity to control many vital functions within their own bodies, such as muscle tension, muscle relaxation, rate of breathing, heart rate, blood flow to different parts of the body, levels of pain, brain waves, body temperature, and how rapidly they heal. Children can accomplish some amazing things if they learn to communicate effectively with their own body, show respect for their body, think positively into different body parts, and tell their body what they want it to do.

When children listen closely to the feelings or signals their body sends them, they recognize that their body can tell them lots of important things. If they send clear, positive messages to their body they will discover how responsive their body can be. In short, if children learn to listen to their body, their body will tell them exactly how it feels, and if they learn to communicate with their body, they can make it do what they want it to do. Many paths of communication are opened through mind-body and body-mind connections. Some simple activities to help children begin to tune into their own body senses include the following.

Talking to Muscles on the Move

Go for a walk (or easy run) with your children and, while they are walking, play some focusing games along the way. Ask them to talk to their arms so they swing loose like cooked spaghetti. Ask them to focus on "feeling" the bottom of each foot as it touches and pushes off the ground. Ask them to stretch each leg out in front of them as they move forward, taking easy, floating, giant steps. Ask them to shake their arms and shoulders and let them go limp and relaxed while they continue walking. See if they can shift their focus to the feeling of breathing slowly and easily. See if they can breathe slowly and easily with their diaphragm (Jelly Belly). Walk a little faster, or skip, or jog. See if they can still breathe slowly and easily. If not, slow everything down until they are able to breathe slowly and easily.

Run together with the children until they are puffing a bit, then slow right down and see if they can feel their own heart pumping. Ask them to focus on the feeling in their chest, or on the vibrations that accompany each beat of their heart. If they can't feel this, suggest that they place the palm of their hand firmly on the left side of their chest just over their heart. Ask them to "feel" the powerful beat of their heart. Encourage them to breathe slowly and easily, to "think into" their heart so that it slows down, pumps easier and rests more between beats.

While walking up a hill or up stairs, ask the children to place one hand on the front of each thigh (upper leg). See if they can feel their thigh muscles contract (get firm or hard) as they put weight on that leg and push down off the ground. As they continue to walk up the hill, suggest that they "think power" into those leg muscles, by saying "strong, strong," as they push down with each leg. Let them see what happens. Let them experience how it feels. Let them share how their body felt and reacted to thinking "strong." Children benefit from practicing many focusing exercises on the move, for example, while walking, running, skipping, playing games or sports, cycling, skating, skiing or swimming. They gain power by thinking powerful thoughts and reduce tension in their bodies by reminding themselves to relax while they are engaged in activities.

Think into your own shoulders right now. Let them drop down a little. Relax. That's better. Remind children to do the same thing when they are reading, walking, running, biking, competing or playing games. Ask them to relax their arms, legs, shoulders, neck, jaw, back and breathing. Ask them to focus on feeling their body move freely. Encourage them to experiment with words and images, like "relax," "float," "loose," "stretch," "easy," "power," "explode" or "strong." There are lots of opportunities for children to talk to muscles on the move that can help them feel better, perform better and enjoy more.

Feeling Your Body Move or Be Moved

Children can develop a sense of "feel" for various movements by closing their eyes, shutting off outside input and focusing only on the feelings in their body. Cross-country skiers sometimes ski in the dark to really tune in to the feel of their body. Paddlers sometimes paddle with their eyes closed to experience a greater awareness of their body pulling the paddle through the water.

To give children a greater sense of "feel" they can try simple movements with eyes closed, such as walking, jogging or moving through a simple obstacle course. It is best to begin this exercise arm-in-arm with one partner leading the way (with eyes open) while the other partner focuses on feelings (with eyes closed). Pick safe, wide-open areas to do these exercises and do them with a friend who can ensure the path is clear.

Super-Awareness Outings

Super-awareness outings are especially joyful when walking or running through trails in the woods or on long stretches of open beach. The goal of these outings is to really open up your senses to see everything, hear everything, feel everything and enjoy everything.

See the trees, flowers, leaves, water, sand, butterflies, small bugs, roots, rocks, shells, colors and shadows.

Hear the birds, wind, water, waves and leaves.

Feel the warmth of the sun, the coolness of the shade, the breeze on your body, the movements within your body and the feel of your own contact with the earth.

Enjoy it all.

You can find extraordinary beauty in "normal" outings and experiences when you open yourself to their offerings, whether it be in outdoor markets, flower gardens, parks, festivals, airports or city streets. The challenge is to open your senses to the treasures within and see how much you can take in while you are out there.

The magnificence of a beautiful place, a sparkling lake or a gentle face can continue to give joy, whether you see it once or a thousand times. Super-awareness outings are special times to tune in, make new discoveries or rediscover simple joys that may have slipped away.

Focus on Fire

This activity works best in front of a fireplace or campfire. Sit close enough to the fire to feel the warmth and the texture of the flames. Focus on following the dance of the flames. Close your eyes and listen to the sound of the fire. Feel the heat on your face and hands. Watch the fire dance through your closed eyelids. Open your eyes and try to watch, hear and feel the fire at the same time. Focus on the inner feelings that the fire generates within you. Focus, relax and enjoy.

Multiple Focusing

Some challenges require shifting focus back and forth from one thing to another, or an awareness of more than one thing at the same time. For a simple exercise in shifting focus, let the children begin by focusing only on their breathing. Then start reading them a story and ask them to shift their full focus to listening to the story. Then ask them to focus only their breathing. Then shift to a full focus on the story. Finally ask them to try to keep count of their breathing and keep track of the story, at the same time.

Some other possibilities for practicing multiple focusing include listening, reading or playing a game while counting breaths, eye blinks or the number of times you swallow. The objective here is to tune in to what you are doing, and to also tune in to a second signal such as easy breathing. If you lose count of your second focus, simply pick up where you left off (e.g., last easy breath you remember).

Heart rates also provide an excellent opportunity for dual focusing exercises. Find your own pulse rate right now. Try to count how many times it beats while reading the rest of this page. Are you keeping track of your heart rate while you are reading this? As long as your heart keeps beating you can keep focusing. If it stops beating for more than a minute focusing is no longer necessary. How did you do? Was it possible to focus on two things that required your attention at the same time?

Relax, slow everything down. There are times to focus fully on the task at hand, for example, when listening, studying, playing or performing. There are also times when it is best to take a mental break or "time-out" to relax your focus—for example, when fatigued, during breaks in the action, when there is no need to focus, or when searching for creative solutions. At these times, letting your thoughts and images drift, or clearing your mind from the need to focus, serves a very important role. Take a little mental break now, so you are really ready to get the most out of the rest of your day.

Great Focus Exercise

Some of the best focusing exercises we have created for children are presented on our audio-tape, *Focusing and Positive Thinking Activities for Children and Youth* (see Resource section).

In one of these focusing exercises two people tell different stories at the same time. Children are asked to focus on listening to only one voice and to then recount that story in detail when the tape stops. The children really enjoy this activity and it is an excellent exercise in focusing. You can do this exercise on your own by having two people read from different books at the same time, at about the same volume. It helps if the material you read has some relevance to living in positive ways. ❤

7

Activities for Shifting Focus

How can you shift focus from something bad (negative) to something good (positive)?

Write it down. Put it in a helium balloon and let it float away. (7-year-old)

Have a highlight to make you forget the lowlight. (8-year-old)

Look for the bright side even if there's only a tiny good side of it. (10-year-old)

If it's a little worry throw it away. If it's a big worry share your feelings about it. (11-year-old)

I put away my little worries in a little worry jug and my big worries in a big worry jug and think about happy things. (9-year-old)

When my friend farted out loud in class I told him 'It doesn't matter, everyone farts some time in their life—just hold your nose.' (7-year-old)

Shifting focus from negative to positive is one of the most important and least practiced of all human skills. Some simple ways to help children improve their skills at shifting focus are discussed in this chapter. The immediate goal of these activities is to provide children with experiences that help them learn to focus and shift focus, at will. The long-range goal is to teach children to: (1) focus fully in the moment (in joyful, constructive, positive, uplifting and helpful ways), and (2) shift focus from negative to positive, or from destructive to constructive, in a variety of situations. Try these activities with your children, adjusting to meet their individual needs, and let the children create some of their own activities to practice focusing and shifting focus.

Outdoor Focusing

Go with your children to an outdoor setting. Sit down quietly together, close your eyes and listen to the "surrounding sounds." Identify the sounds you hear. Pick two of those sounds for a game of shifting focus, preferably the two most vivid and continuous sounds you hear. On my last outing the two best sounds were crickets and the wind. Begin by saying "Shh, listen to the sound of the crickets" (for 10-15 seconds). "Now shift focus. Listen to the sounds of the wind rustling the leaves on the trees" (for 10-15 seconds). "Shift back to the crickets." Other options include shifting focus back and forth from the sound of waves, to the sound of birds or from sights to sounds.

Ask the children to: look very closely at a single blade of grass. Then shift focus to the sound of the wind, waves or birds. Then shift focus back to the blade of grass. Look at a whole tree, trying to see its overall shape and all its leaves (the big picture). Then shift focus by zooming in on one leaf on that tree. Then shift focus back to the whole tree. See if you can shift focus from looking at the leaves on the tree to hearing the sound of the leaves moving on the tree. Children enjoy this exercise in focusing in an outdoor setting and many are able to become totally absorbed in one thing, and then totally absorbed in another.

Indoor Focusing

Sit quietly with the children in the kitchen, living room or classroom. Ask them to close their eyes and listen to the surrounding sounds. Pick two sounds to focus on. For example, focus on the humming sound of the fridge (for 10-15 seconds); then shift focus to another sound such as a ticking clock, fan or air conditioner (for 10-15 seconds); then shift back to the original sound.

Together with the children, pick an object directly in front of them to focus on, as well a second object further away across the room (or out the window). Ask them to focus on the object directly in front of them, for example, something on the table; then shift focus to the object further away, for example, something on the wall or a tree outside the window. Then shift back to the original object.

Shifting Sounds

For this activity you need a couple of helpers who can read. Two readers read out loud, at the same time, while the listeners do the exercise in shifting focus. For example, one person reads a children's story while the other person reads another story or nursery rhyme, preferably at about the same volume. The listeners attempt to focus on listening only to one story, then shift focus to the other story, then shift back to the original story.

Play some music and turn on the radio or television at the same time, at about the same volume. Ask the children to focus on listening to the music, or the words in the song. Then shift focus to listening to the television, then shift back to the music.

Helpful Hugs

Full, absorbing, open-armed hugs are a wonderful medium for shifting focus, especially when feeling insecure, vulnerable, worried, upset or scared. When absorbed in a warm embrace, a sense of security replaces feelings of anxiety or insecurity. Hugging sends signals of love, support and genuine caring. These signals are transferred from your mind through your body to their mind through their body. This shifts focus, eases pain and lightens the worry. Genuine loving hugs from the heart benefit both the hugger and the "huggee."

To gain the most from hugs, focus fully on the sensations of connection. Enjoy the feelings that are generated within you. Never rush hugs. Take your time. Hold on to good hugs. Stretch them out. Soak in the good feelings they offer. Hug a friend, family member, loved one or favorite pet today, and hold on to the hug for twice as long as usual. Do the same tomorrow and tomorrow and tomorrow.

Moving Options

The purpose of this exercise is to give children practice at shifting focus while they are engaging in a physical activity, such as walking, running, dancing, skating, skiing, cycling or paddling. Ask the children to focus on the sounds of their movement, for example, the sound of their feet making contact with the ground, their skates cutting the ice, their skis gliding over the snow, their tires rolling on the pavement, their gears changing, their paddle breaking through the water. Then ask the children to shift focus, for example, from the sound of their movement to the feel of their legs, to the feel of their feet, to the feel of their arms, to the feel of their breathing, to the feel within their body when repeating "relax," "smooth," "float" or "strong."

Ask them to pick a physical skill to focus on (a move, trick, run, routine, exercise or sequence). "See if you can be totally focused on what you are doing or totally connected to your performance. Then relax your focus, and let your thoughts drift away from your performance to something relaxing."

Throwing Away Tension and Pain

It is remarkable how good children can get at letting go of tension or pain, especially if it is precipitated by stress. A 7-year-old girl who had learned to relax using "spaghetti toes" was on her way to the dentist. Before she went I said to her, "When you are in the dentist's big chair, if ever you start to get a little tense, focus on your hands—let them go limp like soft spaghetti." She did get a little tense when the dentist was about to give her a needle and when he started drilling her tooth, but she was able to let go of the tension and regain control by relaxing. She said, "I just told my hands to go limp and relax like spaghetti, and I sunk into the big chair and it really worked."

On another occasion a 7-year-old boy said, "I have a pain in my tummy." I asked, "Where do you feel the pain?" He said, "Here" (pointing to the front of his stomach). I asked, "How big is it?" He said, "This big" (making a circle with his hands about the size of an orange). "What color is it?" He responded, "Red." I said, "Try to make it smaller," and waited a few moments. "Is it smaller now?" He said, "Yes, but it's stronger." "Okay, then try to make it into a ball and shoot it out of your body." I waited about five seconds and asked, "Did it work?" He said, "Yeah, but it hit the ceiling and bounced back in." I smiled and asked, "What color is it now?" "Blue," he said, "but blue doesn't hurt as much."

One night I walked into my daughter's bedroom and sat on the foot of her bed in a darkened room. She said she had a stomach ache. Before I had time to comment, I saw the shadow of her arm wind up and move rapidly in my direction. She yelled, "Watch out!" I ducked in the darkness, thinking that something was going to clobber me. Nothing struck me, and I didn't hear anything hit the wall. I asked, "What were you doing?" She said, "Oh, I was just throwing away the pain and I didn't want it to hit you."

One morning several months later at the breakfast table, she again said she had a pain in her stomach. Where? "Just in front of my belly button." How big? "About the size of an apple." What color? "Red." I sat silently for a moment and said, "Maybe you can try to throw it out of your body." She responded, "I already did. It's gone."

Another child who had learned about throwing away worries was beginning to feel sick to her stomach due to worry about not completing a school task on time. She placed her hand flat on her stomach to take away the worry and then put her hand out the car window to get rid of it. She then replaced her hand on her stomach and again stuck it back out the window. I wondered aloud, "why?" She explained to me that the first time she put her hand out the window there was still a little bit of worry left in her stomach, so she put her hand back on her stomach. But when she did that, all the worry that she had initially removed went back into her stomach. The second time she removed her hand from her stomach, she was able to remove all the worry and throw it away. The striking point is that imaginary acts such as throwing away tension or worry can have a very real effect on a child's body and feelings.

Sticks and Stones

As a child I remember hearing the rhyme "Sticks and stones can break my bones, but names will never hurt me." Rhymes such as this can be useful if children clearly understand their meaning and it serves to remind them that: (1) you do not have to become upset over the words or expressions of others, (2) you should consider the source or background of the person from whom these "names" or negative comments emerge, and (3) negative comments or "names" only bother you if you allow them to bother you.

I have used a "sticks and stones" approach to help children cope with certain teachers and fellow students. One child was having a tough time coping with a very negative third grade teacher. This teacher never had a positive word to say, never addressed a child by name and constantly screamed at children. She was the kind of person who might be well suited to working with inanimate objects like pipes or rocks but should never have been allowed to work with children. Unfortunately, there are still a few people like this housed within our schools. A child should not be subjected to this kind of abuse in a school system and we should work diligently to change or remove such teachers. However, if a child is stuck in a situation like this, it is a great strength for him, and a relief for you, to know that he can deal with it.

This particular child was very sensitive and often became upset when yelling was directed at classmates or the class as a whole. He said it was like having "a big monster" hovering over him every day in the class. I asked him if there were any good things he could learn from this teacher. The only good thing he could think of was "how not to treat kids if I ever teach." She doesn't know how to treat kids right. She never learned to be nice on kids' feelings." I suggested that when the teacher yelled, he remind himself, "It's her problem. Why should I get upset because she has a problem? She is the one who never learned how to treat people nicely." I suggested that he try to change channels or refocus by singing a little song to himself: "Sticks and stones can break my bones, but names will never hurt me." He agreed to give it a try.

About a week after our discussion about the "big monster," he came to me and said, "Guess what? I did it! The teacher yelled and made everyone put their heads down on the desk and I sang inside my head, 'sticks and stones can break my bones, but yelling will never hurt me . . . naa na, na na naa.' I'm not going to let her get me upset." I told him that was GREAT and reminded him: "See, you can do it. You can be in control of 'you' even when the monster screams!"

Understanding Intent

It is rare that parents, teachers or coaches are monsters, even though children sometimes think they are. In many cases children become upset because they misinterpret the intent behind a comment or action. For example, when an adult yells at a child, that child may feel the adult thinks she is stupid, disrespects her, dislikes her, hates her, wants to humiliate her or does not want her around. He may in fact like or love the child. The intent of his yelling may be to motivate the child or to deal with his own problems or frustrations which have nothing to do with the child.

I worked with a talented young athlete who wanted to quit her sport because of her coach. She found his yelling very discouraging. She felt "put down," and interpreted his yelling as evidence of his lack of caring and concern for her. In reality this coach cared a great deal for this athlete but never communicated it in an open or positive way. Through his yelling he was trying to help motivate her to be the best she could be. In situations like this it is best if the adult clearly communicates his intent to the child so that she can accurately interpret what his comments really mean. In this case it meant, "I care about you, I'm trying to help you," even though it did not sound like it to this child. It is also important that we work on communicating in more positive ways.

Sometimes one little positive comment or experience can turn a whole day around.

If we can be more positive or help children reinterpret things from a different, more positive point of view, they no longer need to feel anxious or threatened, even though they may still not like a loud voice. "Mommy loves me but Mommy is tired and grumpy today." "The coach is probably doing that because he thinks it will help me learn faster." "The teacher might be yelling to try to get people to be quiet so we can learn something." In addition to understanding intent, it is also important for children to understand that parents, teachers and coaches are also people—and people don't always do everything right.

One elementary school teacher in my district speaks in a loud booming voice. Many of the children who hear her in the halls are afraid of her. Therefore, the first day of class, the first thing she does is tell her students that she has a very loud voice and to not worry about it. "I'm not mad or angry with you and I'm not yelling at you. It's just the way I am. So there's nothing to be afraid of." She tells them one good thing about having a loud voice—they will always be able to hear her. Helping the children to correctly interpret her loud voice right from the beginning makes a huge difference in their level of worry.

Creating Games with Children

Children, teenagers and young adults create some wonderful games when given the opportunity to do so. Draw upon their energy, inspiration and creativity.

The following games provide a sampling of activities created by my students and shared with classmates. Normally they work in groups of five to create new games or adapt existing games. I simply ask them to come up with some fun games to accomplish certain objectives such as teaching cooperation, concentration or positive mental skills. They do the rest. For the following games their objective was to devise some games to help players learn to focus in the face of distractions.

Distracter Simon Says

This game begins like a normal game of Simon Says. A leader (Simon) stands in front of the group and makes various motions with her arms, legs or body. When the leader says "Simon Says, do this," the children follow the movements of Simon. When the leader says "do this" without first saying "Simon Says," the children are supposed to remain motionless.

In the distracter version of Simon Says, several distractions are introduced into the game. Two people (distracters) stand at the front next to Simon and another distracter stands at the back of the room. They try to distract the children by making exaggerated moves that are contrary to what Simon says to do, and by making comments: "Hey, look at me!," "Do what I say," "Follow me," "Don't listen to Simon," "Simon says follow me," "Simon says touch your toe not your elbow" and so on.

Children are instructed to focus only on what Simon says and does, and to disregard the distracters. Their challenge is to listen well and focus only on their target. There is no elimination of children in this game (or any of our games). The goal is to keep everyone actively involved in maintaining or regaining their focus throughout the game.

This Is a Banana

In this activity players sit in a circle of about five to eight people. You need an object to pass around the circle. We call the object a "banana," but it is actually any fruit or object other than a banana. To begin the game the lead person looks at the person on her left, hands him the object and says, "This is a banana." The receiver looks back at the lead person and says,

"A what?" The lead person answers, "A banana." The person who now has the "banana" looks at the person on his left, hands her the object and says, "This is a banana." The new receiver looks back to the person who gave it to her and says, "A what?" That person turns back to the person on his right (in this case the leader) and repeats, "A what?" The leader replies "A banana." He in turn looks back at the person on his left and responds, "A banana." The response, "A banana," is passed all the way back to the person who asked, "A what?"

The question, "A what?," is always returned all the way back to the leader, and her answer ("A banana") is in turn returned all the way back to the asker. Only then does the asker turn to the person on her left, hand him the object and say, "This is a banana." This may sound confusing or distracting but once you give it a try, it becomes clearer and it is lots of fun to play.

To make the game more interesting and challenging a second object is introduced into the game. We call it "an apple" but it is actually any fruit or object other than an apple. The "apple" follows the same procedure as the "banana" except that it is passed to the person on the right. The goal is to try to get both objects moving around the circle in opposite directions and back to the lead person. The toughest focusing challenge is usually experienced by the person who receives both objects at the same time, from opposite directions. That person is usually the one sitting across the circle from the leader.

One strategy we have found effective in helping children maintain focus control throughout the game is for each person to take one deep easy breath before they speak or respond. Everyone in the circle can be encouraged to take their time and to help friends through the challenge.

Focused Story Telling

In this game, one group member attempts to tell a story,

recount a funny or interesting experience, tell a joke or read out loud in the midst of distractions. Once the story is started, two or three people (distracters) begin to call out questions or make comments (e.g., "Where did you get that story?" "What was her name?" "When did it happen?" "I like funny stories." "I know another story like that."). The goal of the story teller is to stay focused on his own story and to continue telling it without interruption. The goal of the listeners is to focus only on listening to the story. The goal of the distracters is to focus on their own task so they do not become distracted by the story. This is a fun activity and it is more challenging to maintain focus than it sounds.

Concentration

Players sit in a circle and keep a common beat by clapping their hands in the following way. Clap both thighs on CON, clap hands together on CEN, clap right hand on left shoulder on TRA and clap left hand on right shoulder on TION. While the beat goes on, a category is called out, such as colors, animals, cars, songs, desserts or fruit. One by one, players call out the name of a color, trying not to repeat a color or miss a beat. If new colors are getting hard to find, others players can help out or that player can call out a new category (e.g., countries, jobs or sports).

Mystery Person

This is a guessing game that works well in groups. Before starting the game, a set of name tags is created, each of which contains the name of a well-known athlete, actor, musician, person, animal or cartoon character with whom all group members are likely to be familiar.

Each child in the group has a name tag placed on his/her

back. His goal is to discover who he is, by asking the remainder of his group, who are huddled together, anything but "Who am I?" To make the game more fun and more active, encourage the guessers to ask questions that the rest of their group acts out. For example, she could ask, "Could you please show me how my mystery person walks, talks, acts, dances, smiles, moves or hugs? Can you say (or sing) something my mystery person usually says (or sings) or show me what she/he usually does?"

The animated version of this game leads to lots of laughs and can be extended to include acting out distinguishing quirks of mystery persons who are actually well-known members of the group who is playing (for example, teammates, classmates, teachers, coaches or family members).

Performing Through Distractions

Provide children with opportunities to perform with distractions. First let them practice a simple skill or performance on their own without distractions, for example, shooting or kicking balls into a net, tossing balls into a garbage can, hitting golf balls, hammering nails or doing a simple routine. Ask them to focus fully in the moment, to let it flow, to imagine and trust they can do it. Then introduce distractions—people watching, evaluating, talking, yelling, moving, clapping or bouncing balls, and challenge the children to focus only on executing a successful shot or movement. See how they do, and let them discuss what kind of focus works best for them.

Big Screen Focus

The purpose of this activity is to give children practice at broadening their focus. This is a very important skill for playing team sports and for seeing group dynamics. While they are walking, running, riding, driving, playing, or looking at something, ask them to try to see the big picture in front of them, the whole screen. For example, while looking down the court, field or play area, walking in the mall or hall, or riding in a vehicle, ask the question, "How wide can you see without turning your head?" Challenge the children to keep their eyes focused ahead but to see everything on both sides, as far out to the sides as possible. See the floor. See all the players. See the big picture. See the details of the landscape on both sides. Let them discuss what they see and how they can widen their vision.

Encourage children to create their own games for improving their best focus and for focusing in the face of distractions. They will come up with some interesting ideas to play with. ❤

8

Personal Performance Enhancement

What can you do to learn, perform or live better?

Focus on one little thing at a time. (7-year-old)

Imagine stuff you want to happen, picture it and feel it in your mind. (9-year-old)

Paint a picture in your mind of you doing it. Then wake up the picture. (8-year-old)

Remind yourself to believe in yourself. (9-year-old)

Think happy thoughts that make you feel good and make you feel you can do anything. (10-year-old)

Think the opposite of bad thoughts. (6-year-old)

Say you're going to have a good day and look for highlights. (7-year-old)

Make yourself feel free. Make yourself feel you can do anything. (8-year-old)

If you really tune in to your homework you will learn better. (12-year-old)

If you focus on the parts you like first, it will help you to do the other parts. (11-year-old)

If you do positive thinking and concentrate, everything will be positive. (9-year-old)

Developing your ability to focus fully on one thing for extended periods of time is a critical mental skill for learning and pursuing excellence in all domains. Children who develop good focusing skills learn more efficiently, do homework more effectively, benefit from what people say and do, and perform closer to their capacity in a variety of situations. Effective focusing is the most important mental skill for enhancing learning and performance.

On a day-to-day basis how can you help children learn to focus more effectively? Begin by challenging them to focus on one simple task and nothing else for short periods of time. For example, "For the next 30 seconds see if you can focus only on . . ."

- reading this
- listening to this
- solving this
- doing this
- learning this
- thinking good things
- imagining positive images
- relaxing

During performance activities, challenge children to focus

fully on specific parts of their performance for specified periods of time. For example, "For the next piece, turn, run or trial, see if you can focus only on . . ."

- being smooth
- following the ball
- rotating your body
- extending your leg
- relaxing your shoulders
- thinking strong
- pulling hard
- freeing yourself to perform

Everyday Focusing Opportunities

There are countless opportunities to practice focusing, shifting focus and relaxing, every day. During normal activities that children engage in, such as reading, playing, practicing or performing, challenge them to focus completely so they will improve their own focusing skills. For example, ask the children to focus *only on doing* their homework, reading, listening, dancing, playing music, tapping a balloon in the air or executing a sport skill for the next 2 minutes. Before they start, tell them that if their focus drifts or shifts to something else, to quickly shift back to the original focus (reading, listening or performing). At the end of the allotted time period ask:

1. Were you able to stay totally focused on doing the activity for the entire 2 minutes? If yes, how did you do it?

2. If not, how many times were you distracted (how many times did you "lose" your focus)?

3. Where did your focus go?

4. About how long did it take you to get refocused back into the activity?

5. How did you get your focus back on track?

6. What might help you stay focused longer or get you back on track faster next time?

7. When you are performing best or feeling best, where is your focus?

Part of your challenge is to help children discover their own "best focus." See how well they can carry this focus into their activities, for how long and whether anything gets in the way of their best focus. Gradually increase the focusing challenge by asking questions such as: How long do you think you can stay fully focused? 10 seconds, one minute, 10 minutes, 30 minutes? The whole run? The whole game? The whole class? The whole homework period? The whole test? The whole discussion?

Challenge children to carry their best focus for progressively longer periods of time. Encourage them to take focusing breaks or time-outs when it might be beneficial. Help the children to see and feel their own progress by pointing out individual improvement, by letting them discuss their own advancement, and perhaps by charting their progress . Be sure to applaud their progress along the way. Set specific focusing goals with the children, for example to fully focus on a specific task for a certain period of time. In some cases it might be helpful for children to clock the actual time (or number of trials) for which they are able to remain focused. Let the children discuss how well they did, when they were most focused, what allowed them to focus well and how they might continue to improve their focusing skills. Full focus can be encouraged or clocked with a stopwatch in a variety of activities such as watching a favorite television program, playing a game, doing homework, listening to people, reading or completing a mundane or difficult task that requires persistence. The key questions that children can be encouraged to answer are: What focus works best for me? How can I extend the time of my best focus? Can I improve my best focus? How?

Focusing in the Face of Distractions

Once children have learned to focus well in a relatively quiet, distraction-free environment, present them with another challenge—to focus in the face of distractions. Children will improve at this very important skill if you create a positive challenge for them to focus on a specific task for a short period of time in the midst of distractions. Gradually increase the focusing challenge: "See if you can fully focus (for a specific period of time) even though there are distractions. See if you can continue to focus when we add more distractions and chaos around you. See how good you can get at focusing only on your play, job, goal or homework no matter what is going on around you."

Remind the children that all the greatest performers (athletes, musicians, dancers, singers, astronauts, surgeons) are great at focusing in the midst of distractions. "They had to learn to focus through distractions, just like you are doing." It is a huge part of what allows people to become great at what they do and to really enjoy living.

Shifting Focus

Effective performance focusing includes developing skills that allow you to shift focus from one thing to another, whenever it may be helpful or whenever you choose to do so. Many situations and challenges can be successfully met if children become competent at shifting focus from negative to positive, from hurtful to helpful, from what is beyond control to what is within control. Children become competent at shifting focus when you help them recognize the value of shifting to a more positive focus and give them practice at doing so. This begins by guiding children to direct very simple shifts in their own focus—for example, from focusing on one object, sound or thought, to another. Children can then begin to challenge themselves to make positive and meaningful shifts in their own thinking. Ask them to see if they can shift:

- from thoughts of personal weaknesses or disadvantages(why I can't) to thoughts of personal strengths and advantages (why I can)

- from negative thinking (I can't do this) to persistent positive thinking (I can, I can, I can)

- from thinking about problems to thinking about solutions

- from worrying about what is beyond control to focusing on what is within control (the present, the job at hand, the step in front of you).

Improving Skills with Imagery

Hockey legend Wayne Gretzky spoke of the power of

repetitive positive imagery in leading his team to the Stanley Cup Championship:

We taped a lot of famous pictures on the locker-room door: Bobby Orr, Potvin, Beliveau, all holding the Stanley Cup. We'd stand back and look at it and envision ourselves doing it. I really believe if you visualize yourself doing something, you can make that image come true. To this day I can still see Beliveau of the Canadiens picking it up and holding it over his head. I must have rehearsed it ten thousand times. And when it came true on that May night in 1984, it was like an electric jolt went up my spine. (Gretzky, 1990: 82, 252)

Alwyn Morris, an Olympic gold medalist, sat on my living room floor imagining an upcoming race. He assumed his paddling position, "pretended" there was a paddle in his hands and moved his arms and shoulders back and forth rhythmically. He was racing in his mind. I timed his "imagined" race to see if his pace was on target, which it was, to the second. When he was about halfway through his "race," my 6-year-old daughter walked into the living room. She surveyed his actions with a quizzical look, turned around, went directly to the broom closet, took out a broomstick, sat down beside him, closed her eyes and started paddling, just as he was doing. At the conclusion of his imagined race I asked him how he had felt. He said he had felt strong and crisp and that everything had gone well. Then I turned to my daughter and asked if she felt like she was really paddling. She said, "Oh yes, I was really paddling, but it was hard because the wind was blowing in my face."

We have used heart rate monitors with children to let them experience the power of their mental images. After the heart rate monitors are connected and turned on we ask the children to sit quietly and imagine different scenes, for example something relaxing, then something exciting or stressful (like a competition or test) and then something relaxing again. Within a few seconds their heart rates can jump or drop 30 beats per minute, just by thinking of a stressful or relaxing image. One young boy in our program was fascinated with how he could remain absolutely still and witness such dramatic changes in his heart rate. At one point it was like a light went on. He excitedly said, "Oh I see, your brain is connected to your heart." Yes, your brain, thoughts and images are connected to everything.

When young figure skaters use the heart rate monitors while doing mental imagery of their skating programs the physiological responses in their bodies are directly related to the images in their head. Their heart rates increase or slow down, sometimes dramatically, based solely on the skating situation they imagine. Even imagining different skills within the skating program can result in different physical reactions (for example rising while standing in front of judges or for difficult jumps and going down when thinking of relaxing or easy stroking).

Images and thoughts have a very direct effect on feelings, emotions and performance. This is why it is important to get our images and thoughts working for us and not against us.

Children are capable of high-quality imagery and they can direct their vivid imaginations towards many beneficial ends. If you encourage children to cultivate their natural imagery capacities, they will develop excellent imagery skills that can be applied in a variety of situations in sport, school, work and life. Here are some ways to help them move along this path.

Feelization

The most powerful imagery for nurturing a positive connection between body and mind for improving performance skills involves "feeling" the execution of the movement in your body as it is being imagined or experienced in your mind. We call this "feelization" because it centers on feeling. When doing feelization imagery sometimes there is a visual image that helps children get into the feeling of the movement; other times there is no visual image at all. The most important part of feelization is that children "feel" as if they are really doing the movement and that the imagined movement is performed well, flawlessly.

When teaching children feelization imagery it often helps if they move their bodies a bit as they imagine or pretend that they are performing the skill perfectly. Partial movement of relevant body parts helps give them a sense of being connected to their body or a feeling of actually doing the skill. For example, if a child is learning to paddle a kayak, he can sit on the ground with a paddle or stick in his hands, with his knees bent (just like he sits in the kayak) and go through the motions of paddling, while imagining the perfect "feel" in his mind and body. If a child is learning to play a piece on the piano she can sit on a bench or chair, close her eyes and move her fingers slightly as she imagines, feels and hears herself play the piece well.

Performance enhancement imagery that focuses on "feeling" sets a positive stage by helping children to experience desired movements, re-experience good moves and perfect performance skills. It speeds up the learning process and helps children focus in ways that enhance performance. Encourage children to "feel" skills in their mind and body before they actually do them in practice sessions and competitions. This will give them a clearer understanding of the feeling and focus they are trying to attain. Let this become a normal way of preparing themselves to achieve their goals. After performances, encourage children to use their imagery skills to recall parts of the performance that were great and to refine parts of the performance that still need improvement.

An important part of learning and benefiting most from quality imagery is helping children to create or draw upon extremely positive or helpful images, for example performance images that are accurate, strong, powerful, flowing, relaxed, confident or awesome. You can help children do this by giving them opportunities to watch great performers in person or on video, and by reminding them (*before* they do their imagery) to remind themselves to try to recreate that feeling within themselves, to "make it awesome."

As children improve their skills at feeling and directing their own performance imagery, they develop a powerful mind-body connection that enables them to perform at a higher level. Positive performance images can also strengthen children's belief in themselves and their own potential, which opens the door to higher levels of excellence.

Shadowing Movement

Modeling or shadowing the actions of others is a very effective and natural way of learning for most children. As an introductory exercise, allow the children to choose someone to observe who walks in an interesting or unique way. Ask them to focus on the way that person moves by watching very closely. Then ask them to imagine they are walking with that person, as if they are inside that person's body, moving as he moves. See if they can close their eyes and recall the feeling of that person walking. Finally ask them to try to walk that way.

Children can practice shadowing movements by working in pairs. One child walks naturally and the partner shadows him, step by step, movement by movement, walking behind him. Then they switch roles. Groups of four or five children can also follow one child's movements. The leading child can be asked to walk normal, walk strong, walk light, walk funny, walk weird, walk tall. Shadowing movements can be turned into an exercise in shifting focus by instructing children to watch and shadow the movements of one person and then to immediately shift focus to another person. It's a good exercise in focusing and in translating an image into action. It's also fun.

Guided Imitation

Children can learn and refine a variety of important performance skills through modeling or imitating the actions of people who excel. By watching their actions, children form an image of that action in their own mind and body. Then they try to execute that action. Through guided imitation you can help children learn and perfect skills more readily by creating a more complete, precise and positive image of the action they are trying to perform. Begin by asking children to watch a skilled performer repeat an action several times, either in person or on video. Ask the children to "watch very closely" and direct their attention to different elements of the action, one element at a time. For example, "watch her legs, arms, back, hips, hands, head." Then ask the children to imagine themselves doing these movements or actions with the skilled performer while continuing to watch him. "Pretend that you are inside that performer doing what he is doing with his arms and legs and body. Imagine that you are in his body going for a ride with him, doing what he is doing and feeling what he is feeling. Carry the image of his actions inside you as you practice and perform these skills today."

Before the children actually try to execute a skill they are working on, remind them to imagine themselves doing it perfectly, feeling themselves do it just like the accomplished performer they watched. Ask them to "make it awesome" in their imagery. In addition to giving children some "feel" for the skill, this image reminds them of what to do and brings their focus into the present—on executing the particular skill. This "awesome" imagery process allows children to learn skills more quickly, to execute skills more precisely and with more confidence. As one 8-year-old told me, "I like to imagine it first, 'cause then I know what I'm supposed to do."

Imitation on the Move

In this activity children follow the movements of a skilled performer while both are actively engaged in the activity. For example, the child may ski, run, paddle or row directly behind a skilled performer and imitate his/her actions along the way. Children literally learn on the move by watching the "model" and integrating those movements into their own actions. This is a very effective way of improving performance skills.

An innovative cross-country ski coach utilized this approach successfully with young cross-country skiers. The youngsters were asked to closely observe the movements of highly skilled cross-country skiers (their stride, gait, arm and leg movements, body and head position), and to then try to imitate the different styles of those skiers. He introduced an imitation contest, where each of the young skiers had a chance to imitate the superstars. The young skiers judged their teammates on who did the best imitation of a particular elite skier. They sometimes also imitated each other and tried to guess, "Who is this skier?"

Video Imagery

Video imagery opens another important door to performance enhancement with children. In this case children watch movements of a highly skilled performer on video. It works best when the same movement is repeated over and over (about 10-15 times). The children are asked to watch the movement carefully, to try to feel themselves doing the movement and to carry that feeling into their own activity in the gym, pool, studio, arena, or onto the playing field. Once the children are in the performance or practice arena, they are asked to recall the image and feeling of that skilled movement a number of times, and then do it.

An interesting study was conducted on the effects of performance imagery with young table tennis players (aged 7-11) attending a sports school in Beijing, China. The players were divided into three equal groups, all of whom devoted two hours a day to improving their table tennis skills. The first group did physical practice for the entire two hours. The second group watched a video of the world's best players for 15 minutes of their two-hour practice time. The third group (video-imagery group) spent 15 minutes during their two-hour practice session watching the same "best players" video, and while watching tried to imagine and feel themselves hit forehand and backhand smashes just like the great players on the video. Before executing their shots in the practice gym, these players tried to recall the movements and feelings they had experienced while watching the video. The players in the video-imagery group made dramatic improvements in both the accuracy and quality of their shots when compared to players in the other two groups. In the National Table Tennis Competition, two of the players in the video-imagery group placed among the top three in the country for their age group. The combination of video and feeling imagery is effective for improving skills in other sports as well, such as golf, tennis, skiing, skating, gymnastics, football, baseball, basketball and hockey.

Regardless of what skill a child wants to learn, (physical, social or mental) skill acquisition can be enhanced through performance enhancement imagery. In their "make-believe" performance, remind children to "feel" themselves executing the skill powerfully, smoothly and fluidly. They should try to make the image "flow" or "dance." The better children learn to control the movement in their make-believe or imagined performance, and the more they "feel" as if they are actually doing the skill flawlessly, the better their real performance will be. Continue to ask them to be awesome in their imagery. Quality imagery influences the real connection between mind and body and also instills a greater sense of belief, literally "making a child believe." Both connection and belief are highly important in real performance.

On a recent canoe-camping trip, my daughter and I were paddling leisurely along a beautiful lake. At one point she stopped paddling, lay back in her seat, propped a canoe pack behind her head and stretched her feet up on to the sides of the canoe. She was very relaxed and comfortable as I continued to paddle up the lake. After about 15 minutes I said to her, "What are you doing?" She looked over her shoulder, smiled and responded, "Oh I'm still paddling—in my mind." A national team athlete who had accompanied us on the trip blurted out from his adjoining canoe, "I thought imagery was supposed to be used to enhance performance, not replace it." We all had a good laugh.

Goal Cards

Helping children set simple individualized goals is an important step towards personal performance enhancement. These goals can be directed towards anything that is deemed worthy of improvement: physical skills, social skills or mental skills—self-confidence, belief, positive thinking, commitment, focus, positive images, mental readiness, distraction control, constructive evaluation, cooperation, relaxation or any area of skill acquisition. Goal cards are one way to help motivate children to focus on pursuing specific goals for self-improvement. To start this process give one goal card (3 x 5 index card) to each child. On one side of the card ask the child to write down

(1) a personal goal, and (2) a simple action(s) that will help her accomplish that goal today. The goal and action plan are normally written down at the beginning of the day (or practice). At the end of the day (or practice) ask the child to reflect upon what she actually did today to help herself reach her goal. She should also note lessons learned about pursuing her goals. This is written on the back of the card.

Sample Card (front side)

My Goal: To be more positive.

My Action Plan: • Look for three highlights today.
                    • Say something positive to myself.
                    • Say something positive to someone else.

Sample Card (back side)

What did I do today to help myself reach my goal?
• I looked for highlights and found three.
• I reminded myself "I can do it" when I wasn't sure.
• I thanked a friend who made me feel good at school.

Any lessons?
• I learned that I can be more positive and feel better by deciding to do it and by following my positive action plan.

Removing Worry from Performances

One of the major factors that interferes with children's performance in sport, school and the performing arts is worry. Worry results in tension and takes the child's focus away from the task at hand. This leads to a less than optimal performance. When children feel scared or stressed before competitions, games, tests or performances, it's almost always because they are afraid they will disappoint someone, or let someone down. They are afraid that if they don't do well, someone important to them will be disappointed, angry or upset. That someone is usually a coach, parent or teacher and sometimes also themselves.

One way to ease worries and enhance performance is for parents, coaches and teachers to assure children that they will not be disappointed in them because of a less than perfect performance. Some children may have difficulty really believing this if their prior experience with a coach, parent or teacher has reflected a contrary message. Personal acceptance, regardless of the performance outcome, is a message that needs repeating.

Children also gain from learning specific strategies that can help them take charge of their own situation, put away worries and free them to focus on their own performance. Writing down or talking about concerns, worries or negative thoughts is one option to consider. Children and adults often experience a sense of relief when they write out their feelings about a particular concern and seal them in an envelop (or diary). It allows them to reflect on an issue, express true feelings about it and then put it away. Writing or talking about important feelings often provides a sense of relief, clarity or closure, even though one may decide to revisit those feelings later.

Another strategy for temporarily relieving pre-performance worry with children is to give them a little bag where they can put their unwanted worries. We call it a worry bag, or stress bag. A brightly colored marble bag that can be pulled tight at the top, a small change purse that zips shut or a wristband with a zipper pocket all work well for this purpose. Whenever unwanted worries arise, children can simply open the worry bag, put in their worries and pull it shut.

A track and field athlete who worried a great deal before track meets used this strategy effectively at competitions. She carried her bright orange stress bag with her onto the track at meets. Before competing she put her worries and doubts into that bag, and then focused on what allowed her to run well. A young gymnast who was really scared about being judged on routines in practice and competitions also used a worry bag effectively. Her worry about "disappointing others" was so strong that she fell off every apparatus when being "judged." However, she was able to do these same routines beautifully in practice, with no falls, when no one was "judging" her. To put away her worries about competing she used a cloth wristband ("wrist bag") that contained a zippered pocket. The week before her competition, if she began to worry, she wrote down her worries and zipped them away in her "wrist bag." When she arrived at the competition site she knew she had a place to put her worries if they surfaced, and this in itself helped her feel more in control. Her wristband really helped in freeing her to focus on things that allowed her to perform well. After about a month I asked her if she had used her worry bag in the last few days. She said, "No, I had no worries to put in there."

Some children who worry about coaches have found it helpful to put the worrisome part of their coach "in the bag" before practices or during competitions. This can be done symbolically or, as one young athlete suggested, pictorially. She placed a small picture of her coach in her worry bag, smiled, and then focused on doing what she came there to do for the rest of the day. Her goal was to put away the negative or judgmental part of her coach and only draw out positive lessons from the coach's comments.

To perform well, children who compete in more than one event need to develop effective strategies to "put away" one event before moving on to the next, regardless of whether they have had a good performance. If they carry a mistake or negative feeling from one event to the next, it will be a long and frustrating day. Some children have learned to put away negative thoughts from the last event in conjunction with putting away their equipment for that event. For example, after uneven parallel bars, a gymnast puts her handgrips in her gym bag and thereby lays that event to rest. She then begins to prepare for the next event by thinking about and imagining the good things she will do on the next event.

Children who perform in many fields need effective ways to put away errors or negative thoughts that surface within the activity, if they are to perform consistently well. For example, they must learn to quickly "put away" less than perfect attempts, responses, movements, plays, shifts, shots, holes, etc., and focus only on what remains within their control. Mistakes made within a performance, game, test or event require rapid strategies for refocusing. One strategy we have found effective is called F & F. It stands for Forget It and Focus—Forget the error and FOCUS ON WHAT YOU CAN DO NOW. Initially, children may have to repeat F & F to themselves a number of times in order to put away the error. They also need something concrete and positive to which they can immediately shift their focus. The best shift in focus is usually to concentrate on executing the next thing they want to do, or to focus on a positive image or feeling of the next thing they are preparing to do.

In some activities there is an opportunity to draw out a lesson before beginning the next move. In this case, the best strategy is the learning triangle. First pull out the lesson (L), if there is one. Once you have extracted the lesson, forget (F) the error, and immediately focus (F) on the next challenge or move. "Lesson—forget it and focus."

To help children keep things in perspective, remind them that everyone makes mistakes, even the greatest of greats. There is no performance that is totally flawless or totally free of errors. There is no perfection, there is only moving towards it. What separates great performers from others is that they do not let errors interrupt the focus or flow of their performance. They move right on to the next thing without dwelling on the mistake, and because they are able to do this, the mistake has very little (if any) effect on the rest of their performance. The mistake may even have a positive side in that it provides an opportunity to draw out a valuable lesson for next time. ❤

9

Helping Children Pursue Balanced Excellence

For children who are interested in embarking upon a path of personal excellence in a specific activity or discipline, consider the following guidelines:

Their Passion—A critical first step on the road to excellence in anything lies in nurturing a passion for the activity. Children must grow to love the activity, enjoy it immensely and want to do it. Healthy passion is not something that can be forced or demanded; it must grow from within and be nurtured.

Your Love—Make sure your children know you love them regardless of how they perform on any given day. Always love them for who they are and not how they perform. When children start to believe that parents or coaches only love them if they perform well, it puts a terrible load on them. Don't add to their load. If they are worried about whether adults will still love or value them at the end of the performance, they become more anxious, less confident, and don't perform as well. Children perform best when they feel valued, supported and feel good about themselves. Free them to perform and enjoy.

Positive Teaching/Coaching—Find a teacher or coach who excels at making children feel confident and valued. It is extremely important that children's teachers/coaches be positive and nurture love and joy for the activity or pursuit. Great coaches treat people with respect. They challenge children in positive ways and show interest in each child as a developing person, not just as a performer. Take the time to assess the "fit" between your child's needs and what the teacher/coach offers. Talk to other parents and children who have been involved in the program to find out what you're getting into. The most important role of a teacher or coach is to nurture children's belief in themselves and joy in the pursuit.

Positive Role Models—Expose your children to positive people who excel at what they do so they can learn by watching them, practicing with them or talking with them. This helps children learn important attitudes, technical skills and mental perspectives, and creates a clearer understanding of the kind of love and commitment required to excel in a chosen pursuit.

Positive Mental Skills—Excellence is largely dependent upon attitude and belief, so make sure your children are given every opportunity to acquire the mental skills and positive perspectives needed for pursuing balanced excellence. Children will avoid many problems later on by developing positive mental skills at an early age. You can help with this process by teaching them the activities in this book and by encouraging specific positive action along the way—Positive Thoughts, Positive Images, Always I Can, Always Opportunities, Look for Lessons, Act on Lessons, Focus, Step by Step. You may also gain from drawing upon the assistance of a qualified mental training consultant who is trained to help children build appropriate mental skills and perspectives for balanced excellence.

Continued Support—Continue to listen closely to your children, to discuss relevant issues and respect their changing needs, whatever they may be. Make sure they continue to be motivated by their own desire to participate rather than from feeling pressured to please others. Support and respect their decisions, from beginning to end. Follow their lead.

Nurturing Self-Esteem

Helping children to develop high levels of self-esteem is one of the most positive, long-lasting and rewarding gifts that parents, teachers and coaches can give children. What you do and say as a parent, teacher or coach has a powerful effect on children's self-esteem. For children to grow into strong and confident individuals they must know in their minds that anything is possible, and at the same time feel in their hearts that they are loved and valued, regardless of what they achieve in any given field or pursuit.

As a parent and teacher you have a wonderful opportunity to influence the lives of children in positive and empowering ways. Use this unique opportunity. Do everything in your power to enhance children's enjoyment, self-respect and self-esteem.

- Respect each child.
- Find their good qualities.
- Value each child as a unique person.
- Communicate in positive ways.
- Acknowledge their contributions.
- Free them to experience the pure joy of the activity or pursuit.

Many activities provide opportunities to give children a positive sense of control over themselves and their lives especially when you involve them in decision-making, actively seek their input, respect their opinions, and incorporate their ideas.

Their input is an important part of their personal development. The more you value their involvement and contributions, the more they will value themselves.

Competition and performance situations can be stressful for many children. Talk with them about their feelings and help them keep things in perspective. Show that you have confidence in their abilities and let them know that you will love them regardless of the outcome of the contest. Encourage children to focus on the task (on doing what *works* for them) rather than on the outcome. Remind them to relax and focus. This will give them their best chance of keeping things in perspective and performing well.

Win or lose, point out the things that went well, identify areas for self-improvement and help children draw out lessons, as building blocks for future success. Following a loss (or perceived loss) it is particularly important to show your support, to acknowledge the effort given, highlight the positives and help children recognize that a loss can be a positive learning experience. Most of all ensure them that their value as a person does not depend on whether they win or lose a contest.

Children do not go out and try to perform poorly or to make mistakes. There is no advantage in being negative with them. It only serves to undermine their self-confidence and make them feel worse.

- Show your support.
- Highlight the positives.
- Help them learn from the experience.
- Identify areas for improvement.
- Encourage them to act on the lessons.
- Keep things in perspective.

Through patience, understanding and a positive attitude you nurture the best in children. Keep your feedback positive, simple and specific. Share the responsibility for learning with the children and encourage them.

Remember that your attitude, words and actions have a profound impact on children. The most important contribution you can make is to build a sense of personal worth within each child. This begins with respect—by parenting, teaching and coaching with respect; by placing value on the process of learning; by nurturing the joy of the experience itself; and by bringing out the best in each child.

Nurturing Positive Mental Skills

There are five key ingredients to successfully teaching positive mental skills to children: (1) keep things simple, (2) repeat often, (3) use lots of positive reminders, (4) practice positive thinking, and (5) live your dreams—one step at a time.

Keep Things Simple—Use clearly understandable words, actions, approaches, strategies, activities and ways of communicating.

Repeat Often—Repeat important messages, reminders, activities and positive perspectives often.

Use Lots of Positive Reminders—Remind children often to make use of their positive thinking, positive imagery, focusing and refocusing skills and stress control strategies. Remind them often of their good points, their progress, their strengths and their unlimited mental and physical capacity. Stick up positive reminders to help children persist in carrying a positive perspective in places where they will be seen on a regular basis—on the wall, mirror, fridge, door, locker, etc.

Practice Positive Thinking—On a daily basis, challenge

yourself to practice positive thinking and encourage your children to do likewise. Think about good things. Think positively. Imagine positive new realities.

❤ *Think About Good Things*

- Think about the good things you experienced today.
- Share some of today's highlights.
- Think about the things you did well.
- Think about the good things you want to do tomorrow.

❤ *Think Positively*

- Talk to yourself positively today.
- Talk to your body in positive, helpful and encouraging ways.
- Be positive with others today.

❤ *Imagine Positive New Realities*

- Imagine yourself doing the things you want to do, the way you would like to do them. Then go out and do them.
- Imagine yourself living some special highlights. Then go out and live them.
- Imagine yourself being totally positive, and confident. Be that way today.

❤ *Live your Dreams One Step at a Time*

- A journey to the farthest reaches of your universe begins with a single step, first mentally, then physically.
- Take that step today.

- Become what you want to be.
- Pursue what you want to do, the way you want to do it.
- Focus on doing it, day-by-day, step-by step, moment-by-moment.
- Take one simple step.
- Enjoy the magic along the way.   ♥

10

Stress Control Activities
for Parents and Teachers

How can kids help parents relax or make them feel better?

Play with them

Bring them some cookies

Do a little pleasure to cheer them up

Give them a big hug

Tell them a joke

Teach them 'floating on clouds' or 'jelly belly'

Tell them about highlights

Give them a happy happy highlight

Ask them to share their highlights when you go home

Let them know you love them and appreciate them

Teach them to let their body go loose and relax

Tell them to lighten up and not worry so much about little things

Do something that makes them forget the bad things and think only about the good things

Tell them it's OK to make mistakes

Teach them to 'tree-it' and be happy

Tell them to stop doing so many things so they can take a breath and relax a bit

What are the things that really lift you, give you joy and add spark or meaning to your life? What are your real loves? Do you spend enough time doing these things? Taking care of your own needs is a first step in adding balance and reducing stress in your life.

Do you take time out to relax? Relaxation is essential for maintaining your health, perspective and sanity. An important part of developing your ability to reduce stress is to become more aware of what makes your body feel good and what makes it feel tense. What do you feel in your body when you start to get anxious or uptight? Do you feel tension in your neck or shoulders? Do you get a headache? Do you feel hot and sweaty? Do you feel tight or queasy in your stomach? Do your legs or hands shake? Does your heart start to beat faster or thump louder? Does your breathing change? Do you feel a pounding in your head? Do you get a runny nose? Do you forget things? Do you feel rushed, controlled, trapped or impatient? What do you experience? Stop and think about it. Knowing your own patterns is a first step in reducing unnecessary stress. As you become aware of your earliest signals of an impending stressful reaction, you can use these signals as a reminder to take a relaxation break, do something you really enjoy or refocus your thoughts.

Letting Yourself Relax

There are many ways to relax. Anything that makes you feel good, calm, peaceful or in control of some part of your life helps you relax. You can relax by doing something joyful or by focusing on different muscles in your body, for example, by relaxing your neck, shoulders, hands or jaw. You can focus on slow, easy breathing, letting yourself relax more fully with each exhalation. You can go to a quiet, peaceful place or imagine yourself relaxing on a beach as the waves wash gently onto the shore. You can get out of the house, office, workplace or turmoil and find some space for yourself. You can go for a walk, listen to relaxing music, sit in front of a fireplace, visit a special friend, go to a beautiful outdoor setting, do some gardening, sew, bake, sing, dance, or stretch out on a rock in the sun. A long, easy walk, an invigorating run, a warm bath with candle light, a hot shower, a good massage, intimate lovemaking or a relaxing Jacuzzi, all have the capacity to shift you away from stress and ease you into a state of pleasurable, rejuvenating relaxation.

When you are able to move from tension to relaxation, two things happen that free you to relax. First, there is a psychological shift in focus away from what is causing the tension or worry. You shift your focus away from work, problems, guilt, worry, negative thoughts, difficult decisions, inadequacies, deadlines, loss or rejection, and shift your focus to something more positive or joyful. This could include absorption in simple pleasures, relaxed breathing, positive images, good feelings, connecting with what you want to do, relaxing muscles, calming sensations within your body, the beauty around you or positive thoughts about your capacity to control your own destiny.

This shift in focus, away from evaluation or worry to something more joyful is accompanied by a physiological relaxation response. Your heart slows down, breathing becomes more relaxed, muscles become less tense and you begin to feel a sense of calmness throughout your being. This overall sense of unwinding, peacefulness and personal control removes tension and puts you back into a more positive frame, mentally and physically.

Relaxing Through Tension

If you take the time to learn to relax, you will be better able to influence the internal environment within your body and better able to adapt to your external environment, both of which put you back in control. Try some of the relaxation exercises on our audio-tape, *Relaxation and Stress Control Activities for Teenagers and Adults* (see Resource section). Allow yourself to get totally absorbed in the music and in the feeling of relaxation so that you relax completely and can also recall this feeling of complete relaxation. One of your goals is to develop your ability to relax to the point that you are able to relax quickly during potentially stressful situations. You can help this happen by using a "cue word" or reminder such as "relax" or "calm." Repeat this word to yourself as you exhale to strengthen the association between the word "relax" and total relaxation in your body. When you are facing a stressful situation, take a deep breath in and as you breathe out repeat to yourself "relax." One-breath relaxation may not render you absolutely tension-free, but you will be less stressed and more in control than you would have otherwise been.

You can start your relaxation training right now. Breathe in slowly . . . breathe out slowly. Stop reading for the next five breaths, and each time you breathe out . . . think to yourself, "relax." Now let your shoulders relax . . . and your neck.

That's better. Scan your body for any other areas of tension and zap those areas with a beam of relaxation. Good!

Set a goal to relax twice a day for the rest of the week. You've already done it once today . . . one more to go. Once you can relax yourself in non-stressful situations, start calling upon your relaxation response in more stressful situations. As you become aware of any personal signals of tension, take a slow, deep breath. Exhale slowly, and think to yourself, "relax," "calm." Shift your focus to something that will allow you to let go of the tension, keep things in perspective, slow down your pace, let your body go free and loose, think positively or connect with something joyful or constructive. Your full focus should be absorbed in something beneficial that you would prefer to be doing or feeling at that moment.

Relaxation Through Physical Activity

Physical activity is one of the best ways to prevent and release the build-up of unhealthy levels of stress. It is an effective way to safeguard your health when faced with ongoing stress that might otherwise lead to its demise. Establishing a regular routine of 20 to 30 minutes of vigorous activity such as brisk walking, running, roller blading, swimming, dancing, cycling or cross-country skiing, can provide a very uplifting experience as well as a healthy outlet for stress.

Exercise of this nature not only has the capacity to lift you mentally, but also stimulates the release of natural chemicals within your body that relax you and leave you feeling relaxed for many hours after the activity. As a result, you feel better, function closer to your capacity and sleep more soundly.

An added benefit of enjoyable physical activity and relaxation is that both give you time away from other demands. Many personal insights surface during quiet times while relaxing, as well as when actively engaged in physical activities that do not require much thought, such as walking along a trail or running along a quiet country road. During these times, issues are clarified, priorities become clearer and creative solutions to personal dilemmas often surface naturally.

Listening to Your Body

If you listen closely to your body it will tell you all sorts of important things, like when you need to rest, when you need stimulation or activity, when you need a break, when you are about to become anxious or depressed, and whether you really want to do something. If you respect what your body tells you and act in positive ways based upon the messages it sends, you will experience less stress and live a healthier and more balanced life. Listening and responding to signals for the need to rest or relax is an important part of this process. Rest plays an essential preventative role in reducing the harmful effects of stress and increases our receptivity to living life's simple joys. Feelings within your body can direct you wisely in living, loving and establishing priorities.

Relaxation Through Sexual Activity

To be most beneficial from a stress reduction perspective, sexual activity should be something that both partners find joyful and worry-free. It should be something you choose to do, want to do, enjoy doing and engage in with a willing, loving partner who is committed to ensuring a mutually pleasurable experience. When entered on these terms, sexual intercourse is the perfect embodiment of a fully focused, heightened state of stimulation, followed by a deep and satisfying sense of complete relaxation. It is one of the most stimulating and most deeply relaxing human experiences.

Protective Force Fields

When entering stressful environments some people find it helpful to imagine that they are surrounded by an invisible protective barrier, or force field, such as you might see on *Star Trek*. This force field can create a sense of personal space and protect you from unwanted intrusions or potentially harmful input. Those who use this protective image effectively remain aware of what is going on around them, but refuse to allow negative comments or potential hassles to get through. Anything negative simply bounces off their protective force field. Only relevant information and positive thoughts are allowed to come through.

Imagine Positive Resolutions

Think of a recent situation where you "lost it," misread the situation, overreacted or lost your positive focus. Think back to that specific incident. Why do you think you reacted the way you did? What do you think you could have done to respond more positively? If you are confronted with a similar situation in the future, how would you prefer to respond?

Once you have thought about what would help you remain calm, positive and effective, try to imagine yourself responding that way in a specific stressful situation that you may face. Imagine yourself preventing the disturbance from arising in the first place or resolving it in a constructive way. The next time you are actually faced with a similar situation, remind yourself to respond in this way.

Running Lessons

I would like to share with you seven lessons for living that have grown out of my own running experiences. I am reminded of at least one of these lessons every time I wind my way up and down the forest trails on which I run.

The First Lesson—Don't make major decisions when you are running up a hill. You will breathe a lot easier when you come over the top. Things look and feel different once you get on even ground or start down the other side of the hill. In many life situations you may be tempted to give up when climbing a difficult hill, but the view over the top is always different, and once there you always seem to gain the perspective and energy needed to continue.

The Second Lesson—Find something positive within the situation you face, no matter how it may appear at first glance. If you are running into the wind, it's good; it keeps you cool and trains you well. If you are running with the wind, it's good; it helps you float along. If there is no wind, it's good; it lets you enjoy the tranquillity of a calm day. If the sun is shining, it's good; it's nice to feel the sun on your face and body. If it's cloudy, it's good; it keeps you a bit cooler. If it's raining, it's good; it's fun to feel the sensation of rain on your body, to splash through puddles and to come into closer contact with elements we often avoid. There is something good in almost every situation if you choose to look for it and commit yourself to find it.

The Third Lesson—Don't run with a pebble in your shoe when you don't have to. Stop and take it out. Deal with the irritant as soon as you become aware of it. You gain not only from removing pebbles from your shoes but also by removing them from other areas of life.

Sometimes when paddling a canoe you ride out of balance, tilted to one side due to the placement of a pack or because of the way you or your partner are positioned. Sometimes you live your life out of balance due to the placement or weighting of your priorities. You can continue to move along in an unbalanced or unjoyful way for hours, days or years, or stop for a moment and shift things into balance. Which makes more sense to you? You decide. Why run or live your life out of balance, or with a pebble in your shoe, when you don't have to?

The Fourth Lesson—Follow your visions and dreams. When you are running to a distant destination, the image of getting there is often all that keeps you going, especially if the path is hard and steep. Hang onto your vision or dream. Refuse to let "reality" get in your way. There are obstacles and hardships along any meaningful path, but the image of your distant destination will guide you through the obstacles, as long as you keep that image up front in your mind. If you have a vision or personal dream and you really want to accomplish it, keep that dream up front in your mind. It is not only a dream but your goal and your guide for getting there.

The Fifth Lesson—Always support yourself and talk to yourself in positive ways. When you are running through challenges, hardships or obstacles, it is especially important to support yourself and talk to yourself in positive ways. Any positive image or statement that is relevant to you can get you through long runs or long days. Sometimes it is the only thing that keeps you going. You have the opportunity to be positive with yourself over and over, a hundred times, a thousand times. When you repeat something positive to yourself often enough, something positive is bound to come out. Any positive repetitive statement that is personally relevant to you can get you through long runs or long days.

The Sixth Lesson—Focus on what is within your control. When running through difficult terrain in the woods you stumble or fall only if you take your focus off the step in front of you. When living your life, obstacles only control you if you fail to focus on what is within your control. Obstacles, barriers or set-backs are what you experience when you take your focus off the step in front of you.

The Seventh Lesson—Move forward step-by-step each day. All things of importance, all worthy goals are accomplished by taking tiny little steps forward each day. There is only the step in front of you—nothing else matters. You are always fully capable of taking one little step. Take that step, and then the next, and the next. This is the path to completing your mission, fulfilling your dream and excelling at living.

Staying on a Positive Path

You can stay on a positive path by doing things that really lift you, by enjoying magic moments and by talking with someone who listens. You can get back on a positive path by reminding yourself to keep things in perspective, and by focusing on the step in front of you.

Every experience is an opportunity to know yourself better, to extend your limits, to test your focus, to stay positive, to enjoy the journey. Make the best of it.

Choose to live fully, learn joyfully and grow in positive ways.

Someone is getting in my way; I suspect that someone is me, or you.

When you fail to take care of your own needs, things get out of perspective. Take care of you.

Take control. Refuse to be controlled in ways that limit you and your personal growth.

You can't control what happened, but you can control what you do next.

The set-back is beyond your control. Recovery is within your control. Focus on the first step of your recovery.

What you do now is most important.

When some options are no longer available, choose the best of the remaining options.

Turn negatives into positives.

Learn from everything you do. Draw out the lessons and live them.

Look for the opportunities. Take advantage of them.

Recognize your own strengths. Make the best of them.

Focus on the doing; let the outcome take care of itself.

Stay relaxed. Go with your feelings. Go with what you know works for you.

Big goals are accomplished by weaving a bunch of little goals together. Focus on the little goals, stitch by stitch.

Focus fully, try your best and know that it's not the end of the world if you don't achieve this objective at this moment.

Believe in yourself through the ups and downs, especially the downs. Support yourself. You deserve it.

Remember, you are competent, skilled, caring and totally worthy of living your hopes and dreams.

The wonderful thing about focusing fully on one thing is that it frees you from everything else.

Enjoy the simple pleasures. Enjoy the simple treasures. Look for the positive side of everything.

Take your time. Have a "slo-mo" moment, morning or day.

Dance with the little things that lift you. Soak in them. Live more magic moments.. ❤

11

Reminders, Reminders, Reminders

How can you be more POSITIVE?

Play in mud puddles. (5-year-old)

Be nice to people. (7-year-old)

Look for things you can do. (7-year-old)

Say I can! (8-year-old)

What things make you FEEL BEST?

Having a very good friend.

Cuddling with my dad.

When I come home after school.

Hugging Mom.

Playing with my kitten.

When I learn new stuff.

When I jump into a cold pool on a hot summer day.

Every human being is capable of developing skills for positive living. These skills are completely within your control. You can think more positively if you commit yourself to do it, because your thoughts are within your control. You can be more supportive with others, more focused, more relaxed, better at coping with stress or better at finding good things in yourself and in each day, if you decide to work at it. All of these things are within your control, and you are the only one who can control them.

The critical question is: Will you act in more positive ways that will enable positive mental skills to become an integral part of your children's lives? The answer will depend upon the extent to which you commit yourself, and remind your children, to think and act in positive and self-fulfilling ways.

I am reminded of the time that my 5-year-old daughter asked me to follow a new road. For a long time I had been taking a bumpy old road. One evening she asked me to take a new road. The new road was smoother, more scenic and better than the old road. There were many good reasons for taking the new road and only one reason for taking the old road—habit. The following morning on the way to drop her off at school, I went right by the turn-off for the new road, without thinking. She said, "How come we didn't take the new road?" Said I, "Sorry, I forgot. I'll take it on the way home after school." But I forgot again.

I was determined to take the new road the next morning—I put a little note up on the door, so I'd see it when I went out, and put a little reminder on the steering wheel. I also asked my daughter to remind me to take the new road, as we approached the turn-off. This worked well.

I was proud of myself for taking the new road every day that week. Then one morning we were running late. We were rushing through everything, trying to get to school on time. We flew out the door, jumped into the car and were clipping along at a pretty good rate. I drove right past the turn-off and followed the old road, as I had done so often in the past. I didn't use a reminder. I didn't think about the best road. I just drove along the trail of habit.

When we are feeling rushed or pressured, we often fall into old habits, even though they may not be best in terms of achieving our ultimate objectives. It takes time to follow a new and better road. It takes persistent reminders to consistently follow a better path. Be patient through this process, with yourself and your children. Expect progress, but don't expect instant miracles.

We are all capable of taking a new road, whether it be with respect to coping with stress, listening attentively, expressing feelings, balancing our lives or providing support for others. All we need is the will to do it and personal reminders to focus us on doing it at the right time. Get into the habit of reminding yourself and your children to act in uplifting ways. This will give everyone the best chance of living positive and balanced lives.

Reminders can include anything that serves to stimulate you and your children to think, act and live in positive and self-fulfilling ways, including pictures, posters, words, phrases, symbols or images. Visual reminders should be vivid, strong, eye-catching and personally meaningful. They should be well placed so that they are easily seen or heard many times each day. For example on mirrors, walls or ceilings, on the television or fridge, on the inside of lockers, in gym bags, on shoes, in books, on equipment or on the inside brim of a baseball cap.

Positive reminders have been used by human beings since the beginning of humankind. Drawings, paintings, carvings, shells, animals, skins, feathers, claws and masks, depicting the strengths and qualities of animals, nature and the universe were used by our original people as symbolic reminders of strength, cooperation, power and positive spirits. This was an attempt to remind people to carry the positive traits, qualities or spirits of these magnificent beings in nature.

In today's world the only reminders that are pumped into children's minds in a systematic and multi-dimensional way are the advertisements that condition them to buy and consume. These reminders are constant, on television, radio, billboards, buses, city streets and country roads, in subways, airports, magazines, comic books, newspapers, movies, shopping malls and at sporting events, *because reminders work.* Imagine what could be achieved if mediums such as these were directed towards improving the quality of human lives.

When teaching children to think and act positively, your support and your reminders are very important. Give the children lots of encouragement every day and set the best example you can for positive thinking and positive living. Think about what makes you feel supported, positive and valued. Help your children feel supported, positive and valued in the same way.

REMINDERS

Be Positive with Yourself and Others

Look For the Good Things in This Day

When You are Here, *Be Here* Totally

Do the Things that *Lift You*

Look For the Sunshine in Each Day

Say No to Unwanted Demands, Say *Yes to Life*

Believe in Your Own Strength and Capacity

Know You Can

Relax—Let the Tension Go

Forget it and Focus on Something within Your Control

Love, Smile, *Enjoy*. ❤

12

Leading the Way

What can parents and teachers do to make you feel positive and confident?

Say that's excellent

Let you know they love you

Credit you

Compliment you

Take you out

Let you have a friend over

Let you do things to show they trust you

Be flexible

Show that they appreciate what you do

Show that they appreciate you

This book has emphasized the importance of helping children

to carry positive perspectives and deal effectively with the stresses of living in today's world. The goal is to help you provide children with healthy life perspectives and specific mental skills that will empower them to live more fully and cope more effectively for life. Here is how you can lead the way.

Introducing Positive Mental Skills

As a parent, you can introduce positive life skills activities to your children at home, either individually or as a family. As a teacher, coach or counselor you can introduce these activities to children in a classroom, gym or outdoors. When presenting a mental skills training program to children it is sometimes helpful to alternate between tranquil activities—for example, those involving imagery, relaxation, focusing—and more active sports or cooperative games. This ensures that children are provided with a healthy physical outlet as well as an opportunity for relaxation.

Whether at home, camp or in school, build an established routine into the presentation of activities. Children like repetition and the security of an established routine. At least some parts of the procedure should be known and followed on a regular basis. This might include when you do it, what you start with and what you end with (for example, start with sharing highlights and end with relaxation). Children really enjoy the audio-taped activities, and benefit from simple, direct ways of communication. They are also motivated by the fact that great athletes and astronauts use these same mental skills and positive perspectives.

Simplicity, repetition, reminders and belief in children's potential should be your guide. Be respectful of children's perspectives and supportive of their progress. Be comforted by the fact that children will become accomplished at using positive mental skills with practice, and as a result they will experience less anxiety, and enjoy a greater sense of personal control over themselves and the situations they face throughout life. Let your efforts be guided by the following seven directives:

Simple Strategies—Use simple approaches that allow children to create a clear image or feeling of what they are trying to accomplish. A child can pretend he is a piece of cooked spaghetti to relax, imagine he is changing channels on a television to change his focus, use a little marble bag ("stress bag") to place worries in, do imagery while watching an accomplished performer execute a skill, or focus on one corn flake and then find it among a number of others. Expand upon simple concepts such as these when working with children.

Keep It Fun—It is very important to maintain an element of fun in your approach. Children have fun pretending they are a piece of cooked spaghetti curling up on a plate, or shaking a bowl of Jell-O for Jelly Belly, or wiggling and then relaxing their eyebrows, tongue or toes. Think of fun ways to introduce concepts and activities. Join in the activities with the children and freely adapt the activities based on their input. Turn "exercises" into fun "games." It is the quickest way into a child's mind and heart.

Be Positive and Hopeful—Children define themselves and their abilities based upon what they see in the mirror you hold up to them. Make sure they see themselves reflected in a positive light. Make sure they feel your belief, love, warmth, acceptance and respect. Make sure they feel free to be themselves, to like themselves, to feel good about themselves and to live magic moments.

Whether you work with children in school, in sport, in camps, at home or in hospital settings, it is important that you project your belief in each child, in his/her strengths, in his/her capacity to overcome obstacles and reach personal goals. Part of your goal is to help children gain a sense of control and belief in themselves so they know that when they set their mind to do something, they can achieve it. This is accomplished by being positive, by looking for opportunities to build their self-confidence and by teaching children that they can direct their own thoughts and actions. Remind children of their strengths and their positive capacities. Help them to remember the good things they do. Recall the times when something went well. Be enthusiastic about their progress. Remind children to think and act in ways that you have both agreed will help them accomplish their personal goals. The more positives you can build into a child's life the stronger and more capable he/she will likely be. Continue to build upon their strengths. This is an important component of any successful life skills program and essential for all those who live or work with children.

Concrete Strategies—Take advantage of everyday opportunities to help children avoid getting unnecessarily upset, and to shorten the time over which they remain upset. Listen to their concerns, share in their feelings and discuss different ways of coping. Encourage children to be physically active in fun-filled ways, and to relax more fully on a regular basis. Help them to distinguish between little things that create unnecessary anxiety and really big life-and-death issues. Help them to recognize the difference between what is within their potential control and what is not. Remind them to shift focus from what is creating stress to something more constructive that reduces or eliminates stress, whenever it may be helpful. Strategies that allow children to act out the removal of stress in positive, concrete ways are effective. For example, children relate well to putting worries in a tree, or worry jar, and then refocusing on something positive—like a highlight. Look for concrete ways to help children become positive, focused, balanced and effective.

Individualized Approach—Getting to know a child as a unique individual is a great advantage in all learning situations. The better you know a child, the better you can understand her specific needs, draw upon her input and adapt your approach to fit the reality of her situation. For example, we worked with a 4-year-old girl who was receiving treatment for a life-threatening cancer. Her mother wanted some relaxation exercises to help her child cope with the painful aspect of her treatment at the hospital. I spoke with the child about what she liked to watch on television, what kind of stories she liked and what kind of pictures she liked to draw, in an attempt to determine what kind of images might work best for her. It turned out that she loved clouds, big white fluffy clouds. So her relaxation centered around floating on a big white fluffy cloud that she directed and controlled. Fortunately for all of us, she made a complete recovery and seven years later is still doing well.

Use Positive Role Models—Children respond well to positive role models. The role model can be anyone who projects positive values or skills, who children admire and respect. If well chosen, a role model can set a positive example to emulate with respect to mental skills, physical skills, a healthy perspective, persistence or any positive value that one might want to acquire. Pick an athlete they know and admire and point out that he or she uses positive thinking, focusing, imagining, relaxing, shifting focus and changing channels, every day. Encourage the children to do the same thing. Challenge them to carry a positive perspective into everything. Show the children videos of respected people or performers in different fields to help them form clear images of values and skills they might like to possess, or positive attitudes they might like to carry.

You also serve as a very important role model for your children. Let them see you act on the positive strategies they are learning, both in the games and outside the games. Share with them the things you find most effective for remaining positive, and for dealing with the stresses in your own life.

Multiple Approaches—If one approach does not work for a particular child, simply try another. Do not view it as a failure but rather as another step on the way to success. As you get to know children better and they begin to understand their options more clearly, approaches that "fit" will become more obvious. This is also where your own creativity and persistence becomes important. By working and playing with children, and sharing discoveries along the way, together you will come up with the best options for relaxation, stress control and staying positive. By applauding progress along the way, children will become progressively more skillful at looking for good things, using their imaginations creatively, changing channels and focusing fully in their pursuits. Keep in mind that simplicity, repetition and reminders make a huge difference in learning skills for positive living. Be persistent. Use your own creativity and continue to remind the children to implement positive strategies they have learned in the program, any time and anywhere the opportunity arises.

Teaching the Feeling Great Program

Getting Started—In order to gain the full benefit from the Feeling Great program, set a plan to introduce various activities to your children on a regular basis. Before each activity begins, encourage your children to listen attentively to your voice or the voice on the audio-tape and to focus on doing what it says to do. Set the stage for a great focus right from the start. Ask them to prepare themselves to relax and listen. Help them to understand that this is *their quiet time*, a special time for them to relax, listen and enjoy.

For some children it helps to let them know that great athletes they admire, great musicians, dancers, surgeons, actors and astronauts all use these skills on a daily basis. In fact, it's one of the main reasons they became great. They learned to focus, to relax, to think positively, to look for good things, to imagine their goals, and to deal effectively with stress and distractions. Tell them that they will be learning the same mental skills that these great performers use. This can help "convince" some children who may initially be reluctant to become fully involved. "I guess if Wayne Gretzky and Michael Jordan do this stuff, its OK for me too." Tell the children why *you* believe these skills are important. Share with them some personal examples of how some of these skills have helped you in the past and how they continue to help you now.

Settling In—When you first start the Feeling Great program with your children they will be embarking on a path that most have never experienced before. It may take a little time for some children to settle into the activities and the overall routine. Initially some children may fidget around or not fully focus on the activity, however with gentle and persistent encouragement to focus on doing what the voice says, the initial distractions will subside and the children will really get into the activities. Day by day, week by week, they will get better and better, more and more relaxed, more and more focused. The longer they participate, the better they will get.

Consistency—Children enjoy a regular "set time" for the Feeling Great activities, each day. They really look forward to this time. Parents often find that after supper or before bedtime is best for doing the activities at home. Teachers often prefer to conduct the program at the start of the day to begin the day on a positive note, or after recess or lunch to settle things down and get the children refocused for positive interaction and effective learning. Once you have established a "best time" for the Feeling Great activities, your children will begin to remind you if it slips your mind, primarily because they really enjoy this time.

Live What You Are Learning—Encourage your children to use the activities they are learning. This is a very important part of the success of the Feeling Great program. Children begin to "excel at living" through practice, application and the refinement of these skills in the real world. After each activity, encourage your children to try that activity on their own, for example, at school, during games and sports, or at home before going to sleep. Whenever a situation arises where relaxation, focusing, imagery or positive thinking may be helpful, remind your children to use the specific mental skills they have learned.

Create an Environment for Feeling Great—The more ways you can reinforce the positive lessons your children are learning, the better. This can be done by creating a positive and supportive environment at home and at school and by setting a higher standard for being human. Encourage your children to highlight their bedrooms, classrooms and play areas with attractive and creative visual reminders for living and interacting in positive ways. Make good use of bulletin boards, posters, mobiles, drawings, pictures, collages, quotes and reminders. Use action oriented materials such as a worry jar, a highlight jar, a tree for "treeing" negative thoughts, and a channel changer. Encourage your children to apply their positive mental skills to the various challenges and experiences they are living. Take your time. Be flexible in your approach. It is not how fast you get there that counts, *but how long your children stay there*, in terms of living the skills they are learning.

Taking Care of Our Children's Needs

The greatest gifts we can bestow upon our children are 1) making them feel competent, loved and valued in their family, their classrooms, on their teams and in their community, and 2) teaching them skills for positive living.

Positive living must become part of our children's living reality. Nothing is more important for our children, our family and our society. To enhance the quality of human life, skills for positive living must be taught to every child in every school and every home. Make every occasion an opportunity to do this.

Surely out of a twenty-four-hour day—1440 minutes—we can find 15 minutes to teach our children the most essential lessons for living joyful, peaceful and productive lives. It is the best investment we will ever make in our children, and in the future. This alone will move us to a higher level of humanity.

As difficult as it may sometimes be, you *must* also take care of your own needs. You are facing multiple demands and will benefit greatly by taking some time for you each day, to relax and do something you enjoy. This will not only lift you and give you a greater sense of personal control, but will also free you to give your best to your children and loved ones. By living a more relaxed and balanced life you will improve the quality of your relationships, enhance your children's lives and experience a higher sense of personal meaning.

Who better than *you* to lead the way?

An Invitation
to Act
on Behalf of the Children

For over ten years we developed and refined an innovative life skills program for children with the goal of increasing their quality of living and learning. This action-oriented program is aimed at positively influencing children's behaviors, attitudes and life skills. The conceptual base of this program originated from a lifetime of study with great performers who excel in sports, the arts, medicine, aerospace . . . and life. Parts of our program were originally introduced to children with life threatening illnesses and refined for use with elementary school children.

Over a period of seven years our children's program was systematically applied and tested with some 3000 elementary school children, aged 4 to 12. A wide range of schools have been involved, including large multi-cultural schools, smaller schools serving middle to upper middle income families, alternative schools and schools serving children with special needs.

The results of our studies have been extremely positive at all age levels and in every type of classroom, particularly with respect to children learning effective skills for stress control, relaxation, positive thinking, focusing, and living in greater harmony within themselves and with others. This program clearly had a positive influence on children's quality of living, quality of learning and quality of interaction with others.

As a result of our children's life skills research program we developed and refined two detailed day-by-day *Curriculum Guides for Teachers*—one for kindergarten through grade 2 and another for grades 3 to 6. These Curriculum Guides are accompanied by individual logbooks for each child. The program is very easy for teachers or parents to implement and is supported by a series of children's audio-taped activities.

The program has implications for all children in that it provides them with practical skills for adapting to multiple demands and maintaining a high quality of life. It is centered on lifelong learning, problem prevention, non-violence, health promotion, personal and social well being, learning how to learn, learning how to cope positively with a constantly changing world, and nurturing positive attitudes that will help to live and prosper in a technological age.

Our initiatives are aimed at serving the humanistic and learning needs of children on a global basis. If we are to attain these important objectives within our community, within our country and within our world, it has to begin with children. Action-oriented education for positive living and learning must become a part of our regular school curriculum. Your voice is an extremely important part of making this happen. Only if dedicated teachers and parents, like yourself, voice your opinions to fellow teachers, parents, principals, educational policy makers and administrators within the school boards, will this become a positive reality.

Index of Activities

Resources

Books

Orlick, T. (1995) *Nice on My Feelings: Nurturing the Best in Children and Parents.* (2nd edition) Carp, Ontario: Creative Bound Inc.

Orlick, T. (1996) *Psyching for Sport: Mental Training for Athletes* Champaign, IL, Human Kinetics Publishers

Orlick, T. and McCaffrey N. (1995) *Feeling Great: Teacher's Lifeskills Curriculum Guide (for kindergarten children to grade 2)* Ottawa, Ontario: Feeling Great, P.O. Box 20395, Ottawa, Ontario, Canada K1N 1A3

Orlick, T. and McCaffrey N. (1995) *Feeling Great: Teacher's Lifeskills Curriculum Guide (for grades 3 - 6)* Ottawa, Ontario: Feeling Great

Orlick, T. and McCaffrey N. (1995) *Feeling Great: Children's Highlight Book (kindergarten to grade 2)* Ottawa, Ontario: Feeling Great

Orlick, T. and McCaffrey N. (1995) *Feeling Great: Children's Highlight Book (grades 3 - 6)* Ottawa, Ontario: Feeling Great

Orlick, T. (1978) *The Cooperative Sports and Games Book.* New York, NY: Pantheon Publishers.

Orlick, T. (1982) *The Second Cooperative Sports and Games Book.* New York, NY: Pantheon Publishers.

Orlick, T. and Botterill, C. (1975) *Every Kid Can Win.* Chicago, IL: Nelson Hall Publishers.

Orlick, T. (1990) *In Pursuit of Excellence: How to Win in Sport and Life Through Mental Training.* Champaign, IL: Leisure Press.

Articles

Bonadie, J. and Orlick, T. (1996). "An Evaluation of a Life Skills Program with Grade 2 Children." *Elementary School Guidance and Counseling Journal.*

Cox, J. and Orlick, T. (1995) "Teaching Life Skills to Elementary School Children" *Journal of Performance Education, 1, 48-61.*

McDonald, J. and Orlick T. (1994) "Excellence in Surgery: Psychological Considerations." *Contemporary Thought on Performance Enhancement.* 3, 13-32.

St. Denis, M. Orlick, T., McCaffrey, N. (1996) "Teaching Children Positive Perspectives." *Elementary School Guidance and Counseling Journal.*

Orlick, T. (1995) "The Wheel of Excellence." *Journal of Performance Education.* 1, 4-25.

Orlick, T. and McCaffrey, N. (1991) "Mental training with children for sport and life." *The Sport Psychologist* 5, 322-334.

Orlick, T. (1986) "Evolution in children's sport." In Weiss and D. Gould (ads.), *Sport for Children and Youth*, pp. 169-178. Champaign, IL: Human Kinetics Publishers.

Orlick, T. (1981) "Positive Socialization Via Cooperative Games." *Developmental Psychology* 17(4), 426-429.

Zhang, L.W., Ma, Q.W., Orlick, T., and Zitzeisberger, L. (1992) "The effect of mental imagery training on performance enhancement with 7-10 year-old children." *The Sport Psychologist* 6, 113, 124.

Audio Tapes

Feeling Great tapes—available through Creative Bound Inc., P.O. Box 424, Carp, Ontario, Canada K0A 1L0:

#1 Relaxation and Life Skills Activities for Children and Youth
#2 Positive Imagery Activities for Children and Youth
#3 Focusing and Positive Thinking Activities for Children and Youth
#4 Relaxation and Stress Control Activities for Teenagers and Adults

Orlick, T. (1990) *In Pursuit of Personal Excellence: Relaxation and Mental Training Excercises for Athletes and Performers.* Ottawa: Feeling Great

Feeling Great Program on audio tapes or CD's by Terry Orlick and Nadeane McCaffrey—available from Creative Bound Inc. or Feeling Great.

Music for Relaxation

Exploring Nature With Music—"Nature's Ballet" and "Harmony" (Dan Gibson). Solitudes Ltd., 1131A Leslie St., Suite 401, Toronto, Ont., Canada M3C 3L8.

"Over My Head" (Ian Tamblin). North Track Records, P.O. Box 68, Station B, Ottawa, Ontario, Canada K1P 6C3.

"The Visit" (Lorenna McKennit). Warner Music Canada Ltd., 1810 Birchmount Rd., Scarborough, Ont., Canada M1P 2J1

"Great Peace—Music for Relaxation" (Robert Martin) Outsound Music, 312 McKay, Winnipeg, Manitoba, Canada R2G ON4

"Shepard Moons" (Enya) Warner Music U.K. Ltd., Warner Music Canada, 1810 Birchmount Rd., Scarborough, Ont., Canada M1P 2J1

Video Tapes

"Beginning Responsibility: How to Be a Good Sport." (Advisor: T. Orlick). Coronet Film and Video, 420 Academy Drive, Northbrook, IL. 60062.

"Building Self Esteem: Coaching the Spirit of Sport." (Advisor/Writer: T. Orlick). Canadian Center for Drug-Free Sport and Coaching Association of Canada, 1600 James Naismith Drive, Gloucester, Ontario, Canada K1B 5N4

"Feeling Great: Children's Voices" (Terry Orlick and Shaunna Taylor). Canadian Sport and Fitness Administration Centre and Media Productions, 1600 James Naismith Drive, Gloucester, Ontario, Canada K1B 5N4

"Visualization: What You See Is What You Get" (Cal Botterill and Terry Orlick). Coaching Association of Canada, 1600 James Naismith Drive, Gloucester, Ontario, Canada K1B 5N4

Note: If you are interested in obtaining all of our resource materials (articles, books, videos and audio tapes) from one source, or are interested in teacher/parent workshops on life skills programs for children and youths, contact

Feeling Great, P.O. Box 20395,
Ottawa, Ontario, Canada K1N 1A3
Tel: (819) 827-6652 Fax: (819) 827-6689.